SNAPSHOTS OF HISTORY VOLUME 2

Courageous Voices of the Rainbow Tribe

Diane —
FOR YOUR LOVE Know —
of everyone you know —
I LOVE You!
Darlene

Darlene K. Bogle

ISBN: 1519251467
ISBN 13: 9781519251466

DEDICATED TO OUR FRIEND LARRY COURTNEY 1945 TO 2014

Larry should really have his own chapter to reveal his full story. His life didn't begin on 9-11-2001, but a big part of it ended with the death of his partner Eugene Clark, in the Twin Towers of New York. Larry worked for LGBTQ equality and survivor benefits from that time until his death in 2014.
A major part of his story was recounted in the book and video by Project Rebirth.
Larry had three children, all of whom accepted him when he finally embraced the realization that he was not just their father, but a gay man. He was one of the many Christian men that I knew who lived as an HIV positive man for almost 25 years.
One of the myths I want to expose is that being HIV+ doesn't always kill you instantly, and that in living, your life is a blessing to many.
Thank you, Larry, for being part of our lives.

WHAT OTHER VOICES HAVE SAID

"Snapshots of History Volume II: Courageous Voices of the Rainbow Tribe" is a dynamic and compelling compendium of narratives of the heart. A worthy and important read comprised of touching and wrenching stories about the deeply spiritual and arduous journey to one's authentic self."

Bishop Yvette Flunder
City of Refuge Oakland, California
A UCC church

Rev. Darlene Bogle is commissioned to make certain that the world hears the stories of dynamic LGBTI individuals who have lived their courageous lives authentically. The powerful voices of these LGBTI movers and shakers can now be heard in these pages so that we can all appreciate the doors they have opened for justice, understanding and love.

I have been enormously happy to personally know some of the individuals whose stories are included in this volume and am grateful that now a greater audience can know their impactful lives and the wonderful contributions they have made for today as well as for future LGBTI people, and their families, friends, faith communities and global communities.

There is a power in telling our stories which is why this is at the heart of the Christian Gospel. Thank you, Rev. Darlene Bogle, for letting these many LGBTI voices continue to tell their stories so powerfully!

Reverend Sandra Turnbull, Author of God's Gay Agenda: Gays and Lesbians in the Bible, Church and Marriage and Pastor of the Glory Center church in Bellflower, California.

There's a phrase you're likely to see or hear in many a UCC (United Church of Christ) church now days: "No matter who you are, or where you are on life's journey, you're welcome here."

This book is chock full of stories and journeys of those who, far too often in the world of Christian churches and congregations, we've profoundly failed to truly see, hear, or even take note of it at all, let alone "welcome."

Perhaps if, over the years, we'd been as diligent in embodying another current UCC slogan - "God is STILL Speaking"- as we've been in our political commitments, and remembered how often, within our own sacred texts, it's at the social edges and margins that such speaking usually occurs. Perhaps we'd have found it at least a *little* harder to ignore such stories, such voices - such people! - for so long.

Darlene Bogle absolutely doesn't ignore them. Rather she seeks them out, and gives us their voices in these pages. Naming their own experiences and their own truths -as people negotiating the hard edge of embracing Christian (and especially Evangelical) faith, while simultaneously affirming sexual and/or gender identities and experiences that have been being stigmatized and marginalized within Christian communities for anywhere from decades to centuries - and/or as people recovering and forging differing spiritual paths on the other side(s) of the often horrific damage inflicted by well meaning (and not so well meaning) family, friends, congregations, ministries and believers- they speak of places and choices that far too many in today's Churches are *still* far too reluctant to acknowledge the reality of, or try to deal with in any thoughtful, sustained and prayerful manner.

I double dare you to listen, pray and reflect on their words- and *not* hear God speaking. Still.

Constance J. Barker
President
Environmental Health Network of CA
Since 1988: Providing Support, Advocacy and
Information for the Chemically and Electrically
Injured and Hypersensitive

ACKNOWLEDGMENTS

I want to thank the people who shared their story, and for the courage they have expressed in choosing to be visible.

To Becky Lake, my life's partner, who gives me the support and encouragement to follow my passion to tell these stories!

Once again:
Special thanks to Karen Winchester for her editorial expertise on this project. Her friendship on the journey is a blessing and a gift.

Also to Kathy Silver, for her help on cover design. You will find more Information at http://www.gagamusings.blogspot.com/. and www.Kat-Silver.blogspot.com

To my cousin Beth Simmons for her work on my photo for the back cover.

And also to my beloved Congregation at First Congregational UCC for their support and extravagant welcome to ALL my tribe. Whoever you are, and wherever you are on life's journey, if you are a person of great faith, or no faith at all, you are welcomed here!

INTRODUCTION

In 2012, I published a book of interviews with older Lesbians, *Snapshots of History through the Lavender Keyhole -- Older Lesbians Share Their Stories*. I wanted to capture short profiles and snapshots of women who had been involved in some significant aspect of history. Many were famous, most were not well known, but their stories had significance. It was, for me, giving a voice to invisible women and bringing them into focus.

So, why a second book called Snapshots of History, Vol II Courageous voices of the Rainbow Tribe? A tribe is a grouping of individuals who share like-minded or family connections. As I started looking for people to interview, my friend Connie C.J. Barker told me of several Transgendered people to reach out to for interviews. Her knowledge has been most valuable in making connections. This book is more inclusive than just women. I have interviewed a pioneer of the Christian/Gay movement; a woman married to a man, yet still out as a lesbian in a Mixed marriage; transsexual stories; a bisexual person, intersexed persons, young gay men, older gay men; Gays and Lesbians who have been to-gether 30 years or longer, all dispelling the myth that Gay unions do not endure the test of time.

I interviewed people of faith, and some who have lost their faith. I have interviews with some who have not found anything in Christianity worth identifying their lives with, and some with a deep hostility toward the word "Christian" and all that they understand that word to mean.

I do not apologize for being a person of deep faith, with a desire to know and make Jesus Christ known through my life and love. I believe we are all children of a loving God and are fully accepted by that God, regardless of our gender or sexual orientation.

I have a dear friend in Bishop Yvette Flunder, who has often said that "we are all welcome at God's Table, and it is a very big table. "Namaste!"

FOREWARD

My Aunt Darlene recently posted a meme of Facebook that read, "Religion should open your heart not close your mind. Love differently." This one statement seemed to encapsulate everything I know about her as a family member, a minister, a feminist, an activist and a writer.

Darlene leads with her heart and lets her mind follow. Each one of Darlene's books has invited us into her journey as a woman coming to terms with her identity as a member of the LGBTQ community and as a Christian.

I have always respected her for living authentically, bravely and without apology for who she is and where she is on the journey.

I will state unequivocally that this admiration includes the time in her life when she was a member of Exodus and other "reparative therapy" movements. Even in this iteration Darlene lived, preached and served in the world with her heart open and a sincere desire to help others.

I don't believe my aunt could be as effective an ally to other members of the LGBTQ community if she hadn't lived her life and beliefs and subsequent growth out loud and in the public eye. It takes bravery to be who you are in the world and it takes extreme bravery to admit that you were wrong. Darlene not only admits that her mind and heart have been changed but she invites us in to her life, and her questions and now her quest to chronicle the journey of others.

I sometimes surprise people when I say that I grew up blessed and sheltered because I shared many of the same experiences of abuse, judgment and betrayal of the subjects in this book.

I say that I am blessed because I had people in my life who presented God to me in a way that lead with love, acceptance, safety and redemption. My first memories of Aunt Darlene are of her taking me to ice cream if I could memorize bible passages. I loved ice cream but I loved the special time I got with an aunt who was interested in me as a person and wanted to talk about what was alive in my heart and who I wanted to be in the world. Aunt Darlene always had me memorize verses that spoke about God's love.

It wasn't until I was much older that I knew that the bible contained verses that were used to condemn others.

I say that I was sheltered because even though my parents are homophobic and were vocal about their beliefs I never internalized their or others hatred or fear.

I like to say that I am in the first generation of queer people who didn't have to have a "coming out story". Because of the people like my Aunt Darlene who came before me, fought for equality and visibility I grew up with a freedom that no one before my generation has enjoyed. If I did hear hate from others I could see it for what it was, their fear and ignorance. I knew that it had nothing to do with me.

My job was to be who I am, love who I love and manifest the love I knew was infinite from the God of my understanding. I was blessed to have an ally and a mentor in my Aunt Darlene.

The world is changing. It's changing fast and for the better and everyone in my generation and the generations after me have activists, loud-mouths and "flaunters" (as Freda Smith was called, simply for being who she was) to thank for the quality of our lives. Growing up queer identified in northern California in the nineteen-eighties and nineties with an aunt who in the midst of sharing her journey back towards love and full acceptance of herself and God's love was a powerful shelter.

In this book Darlene Bogle continues her work delving into the questions identity and spirituality. She has been a tireless advocate for the LGBTQ community and a powerful voice in the religious community to practice the principles of her faith. This book chronicles the stories of many people ranging in age from 22 years old to over 80 years old. It includes lesbian, bisexual, gay, transgendered and intersexed people and their experience navigating their lives.

Each section includes well researched and informative terms and explanations regarding the LGBTQ community and its people.

Once again Darlene has opened us up to her journey to understand, support and transform the world and its people with her heart leading the way.

This book is not only inspiring to read because of the bravery shown throughout the subject's lives and the vulnerability of their stories. They are telling their stories so we don't have to have them.

My hope is that every young person (especially those in the LGBTQI community) reads this book and acknowledges that we stand on the shoulders of those that come before us. This book is a treasure to us now and all those to come after us.

Roxan McDonald (Author)
Grateful Queer
Proud Niece
Flaunter

CONTENTS

GLOSSARY OF TERMS FOR LESBIAN AND GAY PERSONS

I t is important to understand human sexuality, beyond male and female. "Sex" refers to a biological status and is generally associated with male or female, as indicated by the obvious physical features of each individual.

"Gender" is a set of social, emotional and psychological traits that classify a person as being male or female. When the biological sex and gender are aligned, the term "cisgender" is appropriate.

Separate from sex and gender are attractions and orientation, which vary from person to person.

The most common terms of usage are as follows.

Heterosexual:	A person who has an attraction to the opposite sex. This is approximately 95% of the population.
Homosexual:	A person who identifies as being attracted to the same gender. This occurs in a smaller percentage of the population
Lesbian:	A female who identifies as being emotionally or sexually attracted to women. May or may not have acted on those feelings of attraction.

Gay:	This term can refer to any person, Male or Female who is attracted to the same sex. Most often refers to men who are same sex attracted. May or may not have acted on those feelings of attraction.
Coming Out	Is the term that refers to the acknowledgment and realization that one is attracted to the same sex, and begins to make it known. This is a process that includes self-realization and acknowledgment, then sharing the information with family, friends and the larger community:
Queer:	A term more likely to be used by the younger homosexual community
Dyke:	A derogatory term to refer to a more masculine Lesbian. It was used more at the turn of the 20th century.
Fag:	A derogatory term used to refer to a male homosexual, who is usually more feminine in their appearance
Bisexual:	This is a term for when someone is attracted equally to Men and women. Less than 2% of the population identify as Bisexual.
Asexual:	This is a lack of Sexual attraction to either males or females. These people may experience romantic attractions that may or may not result in an interest in sexual activity. In some cases, they may feel compelled to participate in sexual activity to please a partner or to create a child. Less than 1% of the population will identify as asexual.
Pansexuality:	An attraction to people of either sex, or are open to relationships with people who do not

identify as strictly men or women. This occurs in less than 1% of the population.

Intersex individuals: This occurs in many births where the sexual organs are not clearly defined, and the doctor and parents must try to decide which gender to assign. For many years, most babies were made and raised as female, regardless of their inner gender. These individuals may have any sexual orientation.

I would refer you, my reader to a new release *by Kathy Baldock- 2014; WALKING THE BRIDGELESS CANYON: Repairing the Breach between the Church and the LGBT Community* as a good resource for further understanding of the LGBTQI community.

CHAPTER 1

FREDA SMITH
FEMINIST, TRAILBLAZER AND PIONEER

The focus of Freda's early life and the foundation of her faith were due to the influence of her great-grandmother, Lydia Harriet Smith. She was a pioneer in her own right, a preacher in the Nazarene Church for nearly 50 years. Lydia Harriet Porter-Smith taught Freda and her three siblings about holiness as they were growing up in rural southeastern Idaho, where their Nazarene beliefs were a minority in the Mormon settlement of the day.

Religious beliefs were deeply ingrained at an early age, strictly forbidding the sins of smoking, drinking, dancing, profanity and card playing. Chastity, holiness and frequent Bible Study and prayer filled their home. On Sunday evenings, at <u>Pocatello's Nazarene Church,</u> regular altar calls brought seekers in pursuit of salvation and entire sanctification. What is known as entire sanctification in the holiness movement churches, such as the Church of the Nazarene, the Salvation Army and others, required a genuine desire to be all that God called you to be, and frequent trips to the altar to obtain it.

Freda was no exception to those frequent trips to the altar and determined at an early age that she would either be a preacher or a poet.

After the death of her great-grandmother in 1946 at the age of 87, Freda's family drifted from the Nazarene Church. As a 13-year-old freshman at Pocatello high school, Freda found a place of refuge in the Salvation Army where she enjoyed their passionate preaching and was quite at home with the familiar hymns, and felt their great compassion for the lost and marginalized of society. Their theology of salvation and sanctification was familiar to her.

"I had been invited to the Salvation Army by a friend who rode the school bus with me. To me, she was the image of purity and Christian perfection. We shared prayer, Bible study, and many long walks together.

I knew I loved her as a friend and fellow Christian. It was not until I was nearly 16 years old that I heard myself say: 'I love you,' and suddenly realized that my one desire was to spend my life beside her. I was terrified by my discovery. Although I had no name for it I knew I had to flee this awareness and seek entire sanctification…the 'second work of grace' that promised instant transformation to free one of every desire to sin.

The next week, in January 1952, I left Idaho and went to live with an Aunt and Uncle in Texas. In my effort to seek and to gain understanding, I spent hours in the library reading every book I could find on homosexuality, lesbianism, sodomy and every other perversion.

Homosexuality in the 1950's was condemned as not only sinful, but criminal and defined as a mental illness. Days in the library, gave way to nights on my knees, both at home and in the Salvation Army Citadel where I worshiped.

Finally, at a Dallas, Texas, Salvation Army Conference, I experienced a life-changing outpouring of the Holy Spirit. It filled my heart with one desire—and that above all: to be used by God. To reach 'others only I could reach.' Rising from a prayer of Consecration, I offered myself to become an Officer. Now, surely I would be healed from these feelings.

I filled my life with service to God at the Houston Citadel, preaching in youth open-airs, teaching, serving.... until I determined it was time to return to my family in Idaho.

Once home, I soon discovered that although I had experienced a powerful spiritual calling, I was not healed. Confused, yet determined to deny my nature, I pledged to myself: 'No one can ever know.' I left the church and enrolled in Idaho State College where I majored in Speech/Journalism, stubbornly holding onto an impossible desire to preach. It was like a fire shut up in my bones. The awareness of my differentness made me sensitive to the few others whom I thought were 'like me.'

In December, 1955, scores of individuals in Boise were arrested and sentenced for 'that infamous crime against nature.' The *Boise Statesman* and *Time Magazine* ran major headline articles. The *Idaho Statesman*, in editorials demanded action from prosecutors, the police and the community. 'Crush the monster' and 'This mess must be removed' appeared in the morning papers. Everyone arrested was publicly identified.

At least one was sentenced to life in prison. Careers were destroyed, families devastated and reputations shredded. Along with a multitude of Idaho's homosexual closeted brothers and sisters I left home and family, fearful of discovery and well aware of the rage around us.

I entered into California's closeted, haunted and hunted gay life of the late 1950's and 1960's. When I moved to Sacramento, I spent nearly 20 years within a community that believed we had to hide, lie, and deny our secret selves in order to exist. Most of us were very successful doing so. It was soul-destroying.

I believed that my survival depended on an elaborate camouflage of untruths woven around my life and the lives of the only other people with whom I could really identify. Like the sword of Damocles, truth hung on a slender thread above us, threatening loss of family, reputation, profession, and possibly the right to live as free citizens.

We lied. It was almost a startle reaction against the closeness of strangers.

'What are you going to do this weekend?' they (the world out there) would ask us. We lied. 'Do you have a boyfriend?' We lied singularly and together.

I went to faculty functions at the University of California, Davis with a male gay professor friend. He had to have a date or the questions would start. He gave me his fraternity pin to wear. He would leave his lover of ten years at home when we went out - his lover worked in the University Administration Department. Had they been 'outed' they would both have lost their jobs and their reputations.

Government workers, members of licensed professions, even hair dressers—if found guilty of 'moral turpitude'--could be terminated and have their licenses taken away by law without recourse. Just meeting together socially in out-of-the-way gay bars was fraught with the danger of not knowing who might come in the door, or--as not infrequently happened - a police raid.

It was following a police raid in Los Angeles that our church, the Universal Fellowship of Metropolitan Community Churches, was founded in 1968. I threw away the lies and started to take the risk of telling the truth

As far as I knew I was the only 'out' lesbian in the closeted, Government-dominated, city of Sacramento. In spite of the risks and the fears, I started speaking my truth and for the first time in my adult life I felt what living free could feel like. More than free, I felt as if weights had been lifted from me. I floated as I had as a child when I put off my heavy winter shoes and my suddenly incredibly light feet would fly up way too high for my steps. I joined a small, newly established MCC church in the area.

'Flaunting,' was the word most of the world used in 1968 to describe my freedom, just as 'uppity' had been used a decade earlier. And my uppity, flaunting soul soared toward freedom, whatever the cost.

"We can't use the word '" gay," 'the Sacramento Bee told me when I tried to advertise the church in 1972. After I insisted, the newspaper did use the word, but they put little parenthesis around it to show that they knew better.

A dozen letters to the editor followed. "'They've stolen our word. We can't use "'gay'" anymore.'" What the outraged writers did not know is that the gay community had stolen lots of their words a long time ago and, furthermore, had used them in a hidden language to communicate with each other right in front of them. "'He's in the closet'. 'Are you going to come "out?"' "Is she a member of the family?"' "'He's straight."' We had used dozens of double-meaning words and discreet mannerisms to create a tangled web of quasi-protective camouflage where we could both hide and recognize each other in a hostile, dangerous, world.

Although all of our code words have been outed now and are heard everywhere - that was not the case in 1975 when the compactly muscular but trembling young man on the step below me in front of my church sought my eyes in desperation. "I don't know why I lie."

"I do," I said as I stepped down beside him and reached for his hands. "I do and when you really understand and know the truth, you will be set free."

Thus, I became a political activist in California, working for women's and minority rights. I became a full-fledged feminist, and formed my personal definition of feminism: 'Feminism' is not about changing the gender of who's on top….it is about getting rid of the gender hierarchical order entirely.'

This was a radical approach in the 1970's. The opposition was not only from the straight community, but from within the religious community as well.

"In 1971, I met with Troy Perry, founder of the Metropolitan Community Church, on the steps of California's Capital. We were both chosen to be speakers at a Rally for Assemblyman Willie Brown's 'Consenting Adult' bill to decriminalize our community.

Los Angeles Police Chief Davis had publicly stated weeks prior, that we were all un-apprehended felons and would be treated as such by his Department.

His statement inspired Willie Brown to introduce this legislation. Willie Brown called his bill 'The Gay Anti-lynching Bill.' He explained that, like his people in the South, we couldn't fight for anything else until they stopped lynching us.

"Troy had marched up the River Road to the Capitol from Oakland, and was the gay speaker. I was the feminist speaker representing California State University, Sacramento's city wide Women's Caucus.

My speech that day, 'Freda Smith tells it like it is, is printed in Robert Ridinger's *Historic Speeches and Rhetoric for Gay and Lesbian Rights (1892-2000)* The *Advocate* described it as one of the two most militant addresses given at the rally.

After the rally, Troy told me he wanted me to be part of this church, feminism and all."

It seemed Freda had found in the Metropolitan Community Church, a church where her passion for justice and women's rights could have a platform. She was Sacramento's delegate to the UFMCC 2nd General Conference. It was there, where she "gathered the few women in attendance to meet in a caucus. This was not a common action at the time, and 'Women's Lib' was a derisive term. Men and women in the gay community were mostly isolated and distrustful of one another."

In 1972 Freda was the first woman licensed for ministry by the Universal Fellowship of Metropolitan Community Churches. She had already begun to speak out for women's rights and equality.

Troy and Rev. Jim Sandmire of MCC San Francisco named her Christian Social Action speaker for the first annual conference meeting of all MCC churches. Her theme that year was to challenge this new denomination to be as radical in advocating for women's rights in the world and in the church as they were for advocating for homosexual rights.

"Everyone knew the desire of my heart and my vision for MCC." She states. "It remains so even today."

Early in 1973 Freda **was** unanimously elected to become senior pastor of the MCC in Sacramento. She pastored there for
the next thirty-three years while serving simultaneously as a MCC
Denominational Elder for twenty of those years. Many times she
was away from the church for Fellowship business and visitation
for as much as half of her time. She began to travel around the
country to encourage fledgling churches. "I had an outstanding
staff of deacons and assistant pastors who supported my ministry
with love and loyalty."

The *4th* General Conference, held in 1973 in Atlanta, Georgia,
was a huge turning point for the church and for Freda personally. She was convinced that the language of the by-laws had to be
changed.

As soon as Freda attained acknowledgment on the floor, she
made a motion that the UFMCC bylaws be changed to specifically
include women in every role of the church. She emphasized that
MCC foretold the future, and it was time to state their inclusiveness
without gender identifying language. She knew she would have a
battle on her hands SINCE the majority of clergy and the voting
delegates were men. Almost every Christian church, including the
UFMCC, used masculine language in prayers and references to God.

Freda watched the faces of her male peers and wondered how
the opposition would counter her arguments. She continued with
her motion. "The language in our statement of Faith needs to reflect the fact that women are as much made in the 'image and
likeness' of God as men ARE. The terms we use for and about God
need to reflect that fact."

She sat down. Troy stood and walked to the podium. He indicated that any change in the bylaws would have to be addressed
line by line. - Freda immediately stood and made another motion that every, "he", "him", "man" and "brother" be amended.
The Conference went through every line of the bylaws on that hot

Atlanta day; however, and by the end of the day, the By-laws were changed to include women as equal to our male counterparts.

"I was elected that year to the Board of Elders. That night, in the celebration, I read my narrative poem: "Dear Dora, Dangerous Derek Diesel Dyke." It was later published by the Universal Fellowship of Metropolitan Community Church Press.

Among her notable achievements in advancing gay rights, Freda performed one of the first legal same sex wedding in the United States in 1975! Anthony Sullivan and Richard Adams had met in Los Angeles in 1971, and within a few months were living together. Sullivan, an Australian citizen traveling on a tourist visa, had exhausted all legal options to stay in the United States. The Immigration and Naturalization Service initiated deportation proceedings in April of 1975, but granted him a continuance to file for political asylum on the grounds he would face persecution if he returned to Australia.

Then Sullivan and Adams learned that marriage licenses were being granted to same sex couples in Colorado. They traveled to Colorado and were married on April 21, 1975 by Freda Smith and Robert Sirico, both ordained ministers in the MCC fellowship. After many appeals, the court ruled against them and Sullivan was ordered to leave the United States in September 1985. The couple went to Europe and traveled for a while, secretly returning to the United States. They continued to live illegally in an undisclosed location

In the early 1980s, The AIDS epidemic was another major crisis. No one knew how it was contacted and it was generally viewed as God's judgment on homosexuals. This "gay" disease was condemned from the pulpits of Evangelical preachers across the nation. All the misinformation only brought fear into our community and across the nation. Freda went back to school and became a marriage and family therapist.

When the Sacramento Metropolitan Community Church founded the Sacramento Social Agency: *"Breaking Barriers"* Freda served as the first case manager to get Ryan White grants to help alleviate the trauma in the Sacramento community.

Breaking Barriers is still a leading HIV and women's needs presence and advocate in Sacramento. Freda's greatest conflict revolved around treating all individuals as *Diagnostic Manual* labels rather than children of God.

"I fought against an indifferent world that could not or would not see that HIV was just another virus that caused illness and death, and needed to be treated that way." She declared.

One memorable event occurred in September 1985. She recalls, "I saw the glare of his brass medals reflecting the sun slanting from the window behind me as Lt. Colonel David Eckert stepped into my church office.

I stared. I could not help myself. He stood, almost at attention--all six foot two inches of him—in full uniform. I felt my hand rise to my mouth of its own accord.

Two major Air Force bases flanked the Sacramento city limits, but none of the many military members who attended our MCC worship activities ever wore their uniforms to church. On Sunday's they sat in their civvies--far from where they could be seen from the door-- bodies twisted to hide their faces when it opened.

'David,' I stopped when I saw his eyes. I knew those eyes. That look had become far too familiar. Too often, during the past year, I had seen this same, stunned, almost unfocused gaze. A mysterious, incurable plague was moving through the gay community.

As I pushed my chair away from my desk, David slumped. It was as though the force that had held him erect drained away through the soles of his highly polished, regulation shoes. 'David...' I start-ed again but did not finish. I didn't want to hear him say what I knew he was going to say. I just wanted to reach him. He fell forward.

I knelt before him.

I held him. Silently, I tried to will strength and faith where words could never go.

'I don't want to hear the words. I have no words to give you back.'

David's scent--a mixture of after-shave lotion and breath and tears--was as lilies to me in that moment. But finally the words that had to be said were spoken. "I got the diagnosis. I have AIDS."

'I know. I know.' We curled together and I rocked him back and forth until his face firmed and became military stern once more. I reached for the Kleenex. He wiped his face. I wiped mine. He stood, his shoulders square, his head erect. His steps were sure and quick as he left and remained so from that day on.

Lt. Colonel David Eckerd's funeral was just one of the nearly 300 AIDS related funerals I conducted over the next ten years."

The Aids epidemic hit the LGBTQ community hard. It is es-timated that MCC lost one third of their male members who had been infected before the disease was identified. Freda performed those funerals, often because no other minister would have any-thing to do with AIDS victims.

Freda remembers lying on the beds of many friends who were dying and looking into their eyes, seeing the terror of impending death. She touched them, many of whom had not been touched in months. She felt the enlarged lymph nodes in their necks, prayed with them, and wept with them as she gave them communion. She overcame the fear that kept these men isolated from human touch.

There is an evangelical epidemic of ignorance regarding not only HIV, but the fact that many Gay people are also Christians.

"I've always said, 'Most people are just ignorant. There is a difference between ignorant and stupid. People who are ignorant just don't understand, but they can learn. (pause) Our problem is that the stupid are teaching them".

One person Freda taught was–Michelle Muldrew. She sent Freda an email in 2013 asking forgiveness. "I was the young wife of a preacher, and we spent many a day standing across from your church preaching hell fire and damnation to you and your parishioners and calling on you to repent. We were angry, zealous and self-righteous which is a terrible combination! You on the other hand were gentle, humble and loving. Christ like. You invited us to sit and talk, you invited us to a beautiful anointed service.

I continued my bigoted preaching for many years after but it was hot air. You and your congregation had changed me on the inside though I refused to admit it. I was about 23 then, I am 53 now and for the past 18 years or so I have been a vocal advocate of LGBT rights."

"I have had many such conversations through the years. I believe that God will bring change to someone who is honestly seeking answers. They are just ignorant about the truth of God's love".

Another time Freda encountered a young man working for "Campus Crusade for Christ" during a California State University Sacramento organization event where he was passing out "The Gay Blade," A popular Christian tract back in the early days of opposing homosexuality.

"I was handing out our church's Folder: '*What did Jesus say about Homosexuality?*' Inside of which...naturally...there was nothing!

This young man would discuss scripture with me throughout the day, and add: 'Sister, Satan has given you a STRONG delusion.'

I would smile at him and respond: 'Brother, Satan has given YOU a STRONG delusion.'

Sure enough, several years later he entered my church. People can and do change their attitudes when they see how Jesus loves all God's children.

It has always been my belief that many people who have the desire to argue passionately against homosexuality are dealing with it themselves. I try to treat everyone with courtesy and respect."

Freda believes that the UFMCC "is more relevant than ever!" Freda traveled the world encouraging nearly every MCC church group in the United States, Canada, Australia, Mexico and Great Britain during the twenty years she was on the Board of Elders.

"We were a voice crying in the wilderness, in many areas, the only voice"

"I believe we, the MCC, are still the primary church that actively reaches out into the LGBTQ community. We are the only church where our members are not only supporters of the community but we respond with truth and integrity when asked about what kind of church we are, that we are gay and Christian. No one is in the closet in MCC, and we expect our members to carry the message to enlighten the world! Under the leadership of our

National moderator, Dr. Rev. Elder Nancy Wilson we have become more unified and more effective in social justice issues."

Back in the 1970's Freda started in ministry as a feminist and a champion of women's status within the church and touched many lives through the years. One such individual who wanted to share her story is Marsha Stevens-Pino, Contemporary Christian music pioneer and song writer.

"When I first met Freda, I was attending my first MCC General Conference in Sacramento. Troy Perry had asked me to write a song for the conference, themed 'Free to Be.' I showed up, completely unknown and feeling lost. I thought I would be seen as a half-closeted newbie who thought she could write a song. At the Thursday afternoon talent show, I came to the stage and sang 'Free to Be,' and 'For Those Tears I Died.'

Freda was in the audience and instantly became my most ardent supporter. She told me she would support my music and ministry in every way, but she wanted me to have a 'tent-making job' before I went into music ministry full time. "No fleecing the flock," she said. I needed to be like Paul, who was a tentmaker, which helped to support him on his travels. I finished my nursing degree, and true to her word, she helped me get started. She sent me a letter of recommendation any time I was going to a new city. She was at the General Conference several years later when I received the Purple Grass Award, which was named in her honor.

After Freda had been elected to the Board of Elders, and re-elected five times, this was the conference where she was finally not elected. She stepped down with such grace. She spoke lovingly of the person who had been elected in her place and generously left her 'mantle' -- her position, authority and blessing, as Elijah did for Elisha -- to the new member.

I could see her pain, though, and I was almost afraid to say anything lest it shatter the brave face she was revealing to others. I waited until she was alone, and then walked up to her. She smiled and patted my arm and started to walk on, when God gave me words for her. I looked directly into her eyes, and said, 'They cast their lots for Mathias, but Paul changed the world.' She cried in my arms.

I attended the most recent General Conference, for one day only. I saw so many old friends that I recognized, even from the back. When my eyes fell on Freda, I thought 'Good heavens. She's over 70 years old and still the hottest woman in the room!"

This was the first General Conference where I had not been asked to sing. That evening a woman began to share from the podium that the first song I wrote, 'For those Tears I Died', had carried her through the most horrific time in her life.

I began to softly weep, and wiped the tears from my eyes. Freda saw me and instantly understood. It was that old 'Matthias' thing. She came and laid hands on me and prayed for the NEXT wonderful way that Jesus would use me. She's the best!

Freda's life is best summed up in her own words. "At the end of our lives it's not the awards and recognition we have achieved, but the lives we have impacted along the way for Jesus. My role model in ministry is and always has been Jesus Christ. Everyone else falls short, including me. Christianity in any and every form must be seen and judged only through the words and life of the Living Word."

Freda will continue to advocate for justice for all, even though she has retired as Senior Pastor of MCC Sacramento. As Director of the *Reverend Elder Freda Smith Ministries* she continues to preserve the early history of the LGBTQI church. She–lives in Northern California with her companion, Kathleen. They recently celebrated forty years together, and although Marriage is now legal in California, they choose to honor their 1974 Covenant of Holy Union made between themselves, their God and their Church. "It is not a legal contract. Our covenant is not enforced by law. It is based on our total trust in one another. I believe that the three components of a healthy union are love, honesty and commitment."

"I will continue my support for equality for all within the Gay community until Jesus takes me home and pray that my influence will continue long after I am gone!"

CHAPTER 2

BARBARA PLOURD
MY STORY

This is my story of how I have arrived at my eightieth year, married to a man, yet identified as a Lesbian. I am the woman I am because of who has loved me, and who has failed to love me along the way. I want to share my story in the hope that some reader will see my story and no longer feel alone and abandoned.

My life began in Bakersfield, California, in 1934. My mother wasn't married, and knew she would be condemned if she had an out of wedlock child. She worked with a man who seemed easy to get along with, and asked him to marry her and give me a family name. He agreed, and I was told he was my daddy.

However, that marriage ended after about two years when she came home one day to find him in bed with another woman. Suddenly, Mother, my younger half-sister, Marge, and I were on our way to San Diego. I didn't understand about marriage and divorce, only that we were leaving Daddy. In San Diego, my mother found another man, Fred, to live with, although they didn't marry because he had a wife. My mom insisted we call him Daddy Fred, and to start calling her Mother Ruth.

The country was on the brink of war, and my mother found work as an airplane riveter to support the war effort. The hours were long, and I remember being left with our new daddy Fred, and his 15-year-old son, Fred Jr. I was only very young, but I have vivid recall of being sexually abused by the son.

Fred Jr. lived in an out-building behind the main house. He brought me into his room one night and forced me to get under the blanket at the bottom of his bed. I was confused and scared, not understanding what he was doing. I remember him pulling me up his naked body and forcing a rubbery thing in my mouth. I kept crying and soon he kicked me out of his bed.

My memories of Daddy Fred were also pretty ugly. We were living in Chula Vista, and Fred traveled across the border to Ensenada many times. He told us that we could go with him on "vacation" when he did his business trips. The only restriction was that Marge and I had to take turns, and the trips were often several days in length. It was on these trips that he began to sexually abuse me. I cannot recall how many times this happened, but I knew when we went to pick up huge wooden boxes of enchiladas wrapped in corn leaves, I could expect his unwanted touch. It was also about the only time in my childhood that I wasn't hungry, because I got to eat as many enchiladas as I could hold.

Depending on how quickly Daddy Fred could sell the enchiladas, he would make additional trips across the border. My sister Marge and I never talked about the sexual abuse until years later.

Our life changed once more when Daddy Fred and Mother Ruth were broadsided in their car, and Daddy Fred was killed. Part of me was glad he couldn't touch me any longer, and part of me missed the enchiladas! We moved back to Bakersfield and lived with our Grandma. Mother Ruth had her own apartment, and spent most of her time with a close friend we called Aunt Harriet. I went through deep feelings of abandonment, thinking I had done something wrong.

I had a roof over my head, and a bed to sleep in; however, that is where "normal" stopped. Grandma had strange beliefs about health and how food should be prepared. She would prepare enough food and salads with mayonnaise for an entire week. Our school lunches consisted of bologna sandwiches and salad, wrapped in newspaper. The salad would be slimy by the end of the week, and the juice would soak the bread, clear through to the newspaper. This lunch became a lump of goo, and we could not eat it. We stuck the lunch bag into bushes in front of the school, and begged food from the other kids. My heart was once again filled with shame. I longed for the enchiladas even though it meant having to deal with Daddy Fred's abuse. I was hungry most of the time.

Marge and I soon learned that we could climb the fence Grandma had built to keep us in the yard. Grandma always made us go to bed at five pm, sleep until about one am, clean house, then go back to sleep until six am. After we went to bed, we would pretend to sleep until we could hear Grandma snoring. Then, we would sneak out the back door and climb over the fence. We snuck through back yards and alley ways to get to the park three blocks away. The hunger wasn't as bad when we could play on the slides and swing sets, which we did until after dark.

Our adventures came to an end in 1944 when a Hispanic man who had befriended us at the park raped my little sister. We had been playing on the swings and slides, and I didn't even notice she was missing. As it got darker, I got concerned and began to search for her. I couldn't find her, and decided she had gone home without me. It was hours later, that I learned what had happened.

She had been taken to the hospital, and Child Protective Service became involved. Once the courts were involved, Mother Ruth was told that if she didn't provide a home for us, we would become wards of the court. Mother Ruth thought it best that we leave the area for a while, and within days we were picked up by a man friend of hers and taken to Auburn, California. This friend was sick with tuberculosis, and had to stay in the hospital. Mother Ruth stayed with us, and took care of his house along with doing house cleaning and laundry for families in the neighborhood. It soon was evident that she couldn't make enough money to support our family, so she began to look for another alternative.

Mother Ruth made contact with the Bakersfield Baptist Church where my Grandma attended. She asked if they could help find a home for our family. I was resistant to going back to that church because I had been raped a couple years earlier when I was living with Grandma. I used to go over to the church and play in the yard. A janitor at the church spent a long time watching me, and one day took me down the basement to see something fun. I was looking around when he pushed my face against the wall, pulled down my panties and pushed his rubbery thing between my legs from behind. My tears and crying out in pain were not heard by anyone because of the thick stone walls. I only recalled this many years later while doing prayer for healing of memories. All these years later, I suffer panic attacks if I am standing with my back to a room full of people, or if I step into a crowded elevator. Somehow I felt guilty for going to the basement with him, and that it must have been my fault.

I was relieved when the pastor called Mother Ruth and told her that he had found us space in the Southern Baptist Home in

Inglewood, California. Because my sister and I were from a broken home, we qualified to be placed there.

My excitement waned when Mother Ruth told us she could not stay with us. "You'll have lots of new friends." She said with a quick hug. "I'll see you in a couple of weeks." She headed off back to Bakersfield to live with Aunt Harriet. My sense of rejection and abandonment was reinforced as I watched her drive away.

Twice a month she made the trip to spend a couple hours with Marge and me. I was really Homesick and missed living with her. Tears streamed down my cheeks each time she left, and a part of me died inside. I began to wish she wouldn't come to see us because it hurt so much when she left.

This was the pattern for almost four years. Then the ultimate abandonment came like an avalanche. The superintendent of the HOME called Marge and me into his office. We sat down and faced him across his massive desk.

"Your mother is quite ill, and is the hospital in Pasadena. We will need to take you to see her after school today." He paused, "I don't think it will be long before she goes to be with Jesus."

My mind whirled with fearful questions. *Is this my fault because I didn't want her to come back for visits? What is wrong with her? Will she really die?*

He came to get us later that day in his big black car. Almost before we were in the car, he spoke: "I'm very sorry girls. Your mother is dead."

Just like that!

I was overwhelmed with guilt and I knew that somehow I had killed her. Each night, I had terrible dreams that only confirmed to me that I was a bad girl. One night I dreamed that I poured spiders all over her, and she died. Another dream was that she was riding a motorcycle in circles around a pit, and I ran up and pushed her into the pit, and killed her.

Inside, I felt dead, and so lost and alone.

One time some relatives came from Bakersfield to take us back with them for a time. They decided not to keep us because we weren't what they wanted, and shortly thereafter returned us to the HOME.

We remained there for the next several years. My escape was into music. I taught myself to play piano. I also began to write music, which I would share with others. While life at the HOME was not perfect, it gave me the opportunity to feel needed. When I turned 17 the house mother of the younger kids offered me a different opportunity.

She wanted to make me her assistant, and move me to a private room next door to her. The superintendent approved the change, and I was glad to be out of the dorm situation.

I had just turned eighteen when our relationship became more intimate, and we would have conversations late into the night. She often came to me after I was in bed, and would lay with me. I loved her a lot and enjoyed the warmth and love she expressed for me. Her touch progressed to a sexual intimacy, which felt both good and bad, but mostly bad. I was confused about what to do, so I went to the head of the teen department at church and asked for guidance.

Overnight, everything changed. They fired my friend, the housemother, and moved me back to the Teen Department at the HOME. I was told that since I was now eighteen, I had to leave as soon as I graduated.

I didn't know where I would go, or what I could do. I had become active at my High School, and was president of a Christian Youth group. I was active in the Youth for Christ group, and kept myself busy with my music. Upon graduation from high school our youth advisor encouraged me to apply for a music scholarship at Pepperdine College. I joined a singing group, and began to travel with them. Life had become somewhat normal by this time, and I was ready to put my awful childhood behind me.

While I was in my first year of college, I met Billy and we began to date. We enjoyed many interests in common. He was a kind person and I cared deeply for him. I was twenty-three when Billy asked me to marry him. I agreed and finally began to feel loved and wanted. I wouldn't be abandoned if we were married. The first year, I became pregnant with our first son. My husband was a good father, and wanted more children. We had two more babies before I was thirty, a daughter and another son.

Our home was close to the beach, so I combined my love of the water with my newly discovered love of surfing. I had started taking my children to Church on the Way, and soon formed a group called Disciples Surf Club. My husband wasn't interested in this outreach which had developed into a weekly Bible study with kids from the church. He continued to attend Church on Sunday mornings.

One young, athletic woman began to attend the outings at the beach, and I soon fell madly in love with her. Our affair lasted the entire time I directed the Surf club. I felt guilty but I was unable to help my feelings or to stop them. I tried spending more time with couples from the church, and being active with the teenagers. My friend and I talked about needing to stop our love affair, and it seemed the only way this would happen is if she got married. She had been dating a man, and agreed to marry him. I was devastated, and decided to have another child to celebrate and remember our love affair. My husband knew nothing of my struggles and ongoing attractions. I was once again lonely and felt abandoned and suffered horrible depression to the point that I thought it would damage my unborn child. As it turned out, she was fine, and when our daughter was born, I named her after Melody.

I longed to be a good person and not have to deal with these feelings of attraction for a woman. *Am I trying to fill the "mother" void in my life?* That thought often crept in as I lay in bed beside my husband. *I am a bad person and that's why everyone leaves me.*

Silent tears often trickled down my cheeks onto my pillow. Then, I met Regina. She was a compassionate and caring woman who attended my Bible Study and we soon became good friends. After several weeks, I shared the story of my previous love affair. She was a wonderful listener, and I always felt better after our conversations. My husband was happy that I had another mother to spend time with and was encouraging when we both decided to start attending Church on the Way: which is a Foursquare Gospel church. Her three teens soon began to attend with us, and joined the singing group. She was the sponsor and I played piano for the choir. On rehearsal nights, we would arrive early and sit in the car, talking about our lives. Regina began asking questions about my former love affair, when she suddenly turned and kissed me. Her hands slipped up my body in a gently caress.

My brain exploded in passion and panic. "Oh, no. Not again!"

My face burned with a glow of passion, and I was caught up in a full blown love affair. We talked of having to be careful and not expose our feelings because we were both married. Our affair lasted five or six years when suddenly she broke off the affair. She told me that she couldn't continue to have a sexual relationship with me, because the Bible was against that type of behavior. Instead, she wanted for us to just be friends.

I had continued to have a sexual relationship with my husband in order to hide my cheating and adultery. I was so devastated when she said we could not continue our sexual relationship that I completely shut down sexually and would not have sex with my husband. He told me if I didn't get therapy and find out what was wrong, that he would leave me. I was filled with panic and fear of abandonment once more. *How can I be a Christian, a mother, an adulterer and love a woman?"*

I was in my late forties by this time, yet still only a breath away from the horrors of my childhood.

I found a therapist, and Regina agreed to go with me. I was honest with the therapist about my childhood rapes, abandonment, affairs with women and how I preferred my gentle, sweet passionate love of a woman to any sexual contact with my husband. The warmth that my lover gave me was deeply rooted in my longing for my mother's love that had been ripped from my life. I no longer could tolerate a sexual relationship with my husband.

I was conflicted, but that doesn't even begin to explain my struggles. Not only was I betraying my marriage vows, but there were the teachings of my church that homosexuality was a sin. *Did*

God still love me? Had He ever loved me? Why didn't He just take these feeling away? Keeping secrets became more difficult with every passing day. Billy still didn't know about my love affair with Regina, or that it was her touch that I desired. I felt like I was going crazy with this balancing act. Regina and I had agreed to be non-sexual, as that seemed to be hooked into the definition of what was sin. The reality was I was filled with intense passion, even if we did not act on it. We remained the dearest and closest of friends for over 30 years after our affair ended. I tried to become close with a couple women, but they were not who I really longed for, and I always felt depressed and alone. I only wanted one woman, and I was not attracted to Billy. I cared for him, but not in a sexual way, and that was creating an ongoing problem.

To add to the conflict, Regina would invite herself along when I went anywhere with another woman. She told me one night, "Just don't kiss me, and we will be fine!" It confirmed that her attraction to me was still strong, but we were both committed to not go against God and the Bible teachings. I never did try to tempt her or cross that boundary. I would rather have her non-sexual friendship than to have her totally gone from my life.

My emotional state was fragile, and I told Regina on several occasions that I wanted to commit suicide. We made a pact that I would have to first ask her permission before I took any such action. That agreement kept me safe in the dark times, of which there were many. I was no longer tempted by attractions to anyone after her. I continued in therapy for several years. There are others to consider in this account of my secret life. A few years ago I told my children, who were now all adults, of my struggles a few years back. They all told me that they already knew, and that they were fine with things. They all knew and loved Regina, and felt I had suffered enough through the years.

What of God? Would the judgmental God of my past condemn me for my behavior? I am still trying to come to a new understanding of my connection with God. My lack of faith has been a huge loss to me, and I have grieved and been frightened at my unbelief. Still, at age 80, my understanding of a loving God is so far beyond my comprehension, yet I am secure in the knowledge that a Divine Presence cares for me.

It was time for full disclosure with my husband. Of course, my greatest fear was that Billy would leave me. Five years ago, my husband and I began a journey of communication that left me very nervous about the future. We moved to Northern California and I began to attend the Episcopal Church. Together, we went to see Pastor Ann at our new church.

She asked Billy to talk about his feelings. I watched him closely.

"I suppose I should have divorced Barbie long ago, but it seemed best to stay in the marriage." He paused. "I am very angry that she stopped having sexual relations with me. I didn't understand what I had done wrong, that she didn't love me any longer."

I listened to him tell about how hurt he was for all those years. I didn't try to defend myself.

Pastor Ann turned to me. "What do you think about what Billy just said?"

I looked at Billy and tears trickled down my cheeks. "I am so deeply sorry for how I hurt you. You need to know that I didn't choose to be gay."

He mumbled. "I want a divorce right now."

"I know that our marriage was over long ago and if I had known I was gay, I never would have married you." I took a deep breath. "Thank you for giving me our four children. Although our marriage is over and we could get divorced, and you have every right to want that, the fact is I have no place to go." I hesitated, "Can I please stay with you?"

He reached out and took my hand. "You will always be my sweetie. Yes, you can stay." His voice was soft and caring.

Of course, one conversation did not resolve the years of built up resentment. I still did not want to have a sexual relationship with him, although the time of our raging hormones was a faded memory. Our relationship is platonic, and we are best friends. We talk occasionally, and I can tell that he hasn't really forgiven me and that he still resents the loss of intimacy.

On one occasion recently I told him that I didn't blame him, but I didn't know if I could stay in the same house with that resentment hanging in the air. I asked him again, which I have done many times to forgive me for hurting him. I was really so unsure of what was going to happen with our situation because at 80 years old, I am unable to work and care for myself. Billy is 87 and still works with our two sons doing building contract repairs. His health is fragile, and last year he suffered a heart attack. I recognized the signs and got him to the hospital, where they did a double bypass. I am concerned that the summer heat will be too much for him.

Billy knows that I am a lesbian, and will not change to the wife he thinks he had in the past. We don't talk much about this topic any longer, and I keep a low profile with him regarding these matters. We have a daughter who is lesbian, and married to her wife, and that seems to have helped his acceptance of homosexuality.

I have thought long and hard about why I am a lesbian. I don't know if this condition exists, however, think I have "penis-itis", and I still shiver inside and get physically sick when I think about a penis. I remember years ago at the beginning of our marriage, my husband would turn me over so he could enter his penis from behind me. It would hurt, and always make me cry. I never told him that I cried. I never told him of the memory of being raped from behind in the basement of the Baptist Church by the janitor. I never told him about having my face to the wall and feeling that rubbery thing between my legs. I never told him about the fear I lived with every day that if I told someone, the janitor said he would kill my Grandma. I never told anyone, not even my sister.

Years later, I talked to my sister about the rape and said I was beginning to wonder if it really happened. I'll never forget her response. "It really happened, Sis. I know because it happened to me too." I felt really sorry that she had to experience the same horror that still plagued me.

I've often asked myself where God was when all this was happening to my family. I do believe there is a God, but I'm sure it's not the one that was preached about at the Pentecostal church. I don't believe in the rigid God that says to either obey all my laws or you're going to hell. I'm just not sure what to call him or her, but I know there is a Creator that I love with all my heart, and I love that Divine Presence. Lots of feelings of loss, but I continue to seek to know this Creator.

I still grieve terribly over the loss of my Regina. A few years ago I was so depressed that I went to see the family doctor who had treated both Regina and me. I felt safe enough to share the reason for my depression. We talked a long time, and she was very encouraging. Regina had an appointment on the same day, and the doctor shared the concern that she had for me, and told Regina I had told her about our affair. When Regina left the doctor's office, she was very upset and scolded me for talking about it without consulting her.

In retaliation, she told her family about our love affair over 25years after it happened. We had all been very close, and her children were treated as if they were mine. After hearing that we had been lovers, they will have nothing to do with me. She was a dear friend and ex-lover, a brilliant person all her life, but the last time I saw her she didn't know me due to her advanced dementia. I told her good-bye, kissed her on the mouth and left. She died two months later. I still think of her every day, and it breaks my heart.

A deep freedom happened about five years ago when I came out to a priest friend who assists here at St. Nicholas Episcopal in Paradise. I shared my guilt that I had carried all these years for loving a woman.

He looked at me and said, "Barbie, why can't you see that it is okay that you are gay? I am gay and it is all right. God doesn't hate you for being a lesbian."

I pondered his words. "God doesn't hate me. I'm gay!" Immediately years of guilt lifted. I went Home and called everyone in the Church Directory and came out to them. There was not one negative response and everyone told me they loved me.

Billy and I are still finding our way in this mixed marriage. We have frequent conversations about if we should stay married after 57 years or get a divorce. We are still best friends forever and my husband still lives with a lesbian!

INTRODUCTION TO TRANSGENDER STORIES

I am so grateful to the Transgender community, and the following individuals who shared their stories with me. I thought I knew what it meant to be transgender, but soon discovered I didn't have a clue who they were and what they experienced on their journey of discovery.

I never understood why they were included under the LGBT title, because I thought they were not gay. What I have discovered is that many of them are gay, lesbian, or even heterosexual. I listened to dozens of stories of persecution, physical abuse, misunderstanding from parents and families, prostitution and drugs, suicide and homicide, as well as strong stories of faith.

I share the following glossary of terms to provide a framework for understanding these precious children of God. It is good to be aware of these terms, but most are built on different concepts and theories.

The understanding of gender still has tons of flaws, and has built terms dependent on social constraints. Society changes with every generation, creating more room for error as we build upon this shaky pyramid.

Please understand that gender has a wide spectrum, and sexuality for every human being is fluid.

Glossary of Terms

There is no single reason why someone is transgender. God didn't "make a mistake" as some have suggested. This is just one of many aspects of sexuality.

I am including a few definitions to assist in navigating this topic.

Cisgender: Any biological male or female whose aligned gender is based on what society considers appropriate. In a logical sense, cisgender is everything that is not transgender. Cisgender also aligns with gender binary.

Gender: A person's expression and presentation of some combination of masculine and/or feminine characteristics.

Gender Binary: is a reference to what is seen in the majority of our society, the typical masculine male and feminine female. This is a social concept that chooses what gender expression is appropriate for male and female.

Gender identity: A person's personal view of their own gender. One's innermost perception of their gender is often formed over time. Gender is separate from the term, "sex."

Gender Expression: The external presentation or appearance of a person's gender clues. Elements such as mannerisms, clothing, roles, body, and sexual orientation are just a part of what helps others interpret one's gender identity.

Perceived Gender: A person's gender clues that help other people identify their gender. Not all perceived genders are their true gender; there are still plenty of closeted transgender people whose perceived gender is not their personal gender identity.

Pansexual: Trans people can be gay, lesbian, straight, queer, bisexual or Pansexual. Pansexual is sexual attraction, sexual desire, romantic love or emotional attraction toward people of all gender identities and biological sexes.

The *Oxford Dictionary of English* defines pansexuality as, "not limited or inhibited in sexual choice with regard to gender or activity. Sexual Orientation is in reference to a person's sexual attraction toward others. These are commonly used words, but there are more sexual orientation identities that become known as gender identity grows and evolves.

Sexual Orientation: The gender of the people one chooses to form romantic/sexual attachments to. Gender Identity and sexual orientation are very different.

Transgender: People whose gender identity is not adequately described by the sex they were assigned at birth. A transgendered person is any person who feels that their gender is not aligned with the gender binary based on their biological sex.

Many transgender individuals choose to conform to the gender binary. This is where MTF (male to female) and FTM (female to male) transgender comes from since these individuals choose to identify with an opposite sex in reference to their biological sex.

Transition: The process of changing one's gender presentation and or expression to align with one's gender identity. This process involves taking hormones, and can also include top (breast) surgery and /or bottom (genitalia) surgery. Not all transsexuals will have the bottom surgery for a variety of reasons, some of which include the expense and/or lack of coverage from medical providers.

Some categories of Transgender persons.
This is by no means the full list of terms and definitions.

It is good to know these terms to more effectively communicate, but these also can be a source of confusion when it comes to defining gender. There are more terms used in this broad discussion, but the following are some of the more mainstream words you will encounter.

Bi-gender:
This refers to someone who moves between feminine and masculine gender roles.

Drag Queen and King:
This term refers to someone who cross-dresses as a performer. This is also an evolving term that refers to drag culture.

Gender queer:
A transgender who has a gender that does not fit the gender binary concept of what is seen by the majority of people as typical male or female.

Transsexual:
This term is often used as a synonym for transgender. Transgender is the more common term in use today.

This identifies a transgender person who chooses to perform anything permanent toward changing their body to help match with how they feel on the inside (emotions). This could be taking hormones/hormone blockers, breast implants/removal, SRS (sexual reassignment surgery).

A Transsexual is a person who does not identify with the sex they were assigned at birth. Many transsexuals wish to alter their bodies through the use of hormones or surgery. Transsexuals can be male-to-female (MTF) or female to male (FTM)

Transvestite: (Cross-dresser)
A person who wears clothes of the opposite sex is defined as a transvestite. The more preferred term is cross-dresser instead of the old term transvestite. These individuals may not make their preference known in a public venue, and can live for years in that private role.

Many of these Terms are based on materials produced by Gender Queer of Lane County Oregon.2004 by Shaw-Phillips, Glisch-Sanchez, Sakurai. United States Student Association Foundation and from Wikipedia online information

CHAPTER 3

YUNUS COLDMAN
FEMALE TO MALE
TRANSGENDER MALE HETEROSEXUAL

I t has been several years since my path crossed with Eunice at an Evangelical Concerned western region conference in Orange County. This is a highly publicized national Christian and gay organization. It was 2006 when she came into the conference bookstore, bubbling over with excitement. She told me her story of going on line finding our conference, and flying in from New York. She had arrived with less than $30.00 in her pocket, and was dismayed to find out the cost of a taxi ride from the airport exceeded her funds. She explained her situation to the taxi driver, who brought her to the campus for the $30.00 she still had in her pocket.

This African-American woman was hard to miss in this mostly Caucasian environment. She shared about how she needed to be at that conference. She hadn't realized there were Christians who were also gay, and when she discovered them on the website, she felt she needed to meet them. I listened to her account of her trip, and how great she was feeling about being able to attend the conference. "It is a real miracle," she proclaimed.

I introduced myself to her and gave her a big hug. "Welcome to our family!" I sensed a special friendship was being forged that very day. We exchanged phone numbers and promised to keep in touch after the conference.

I made a lot of assumptions at that first meeting. She was obviously a lesbian, and was looking for others like her. She came from a Pentecostal background, and was looking for acceptance in that faith tradition. As I recall this first meeting, I am reminded of how, in my mind, things stay the same, or stay how they were when I last encountered a person.

Each year, <u>Evangelicals Concerned</u> had an annual conference. Each year Eunice attended, still looking like I remembered her. I watched her Facebook postings and celebrated with her when she became ordained as an Interfaith Minister in New York. She studied multiple theologies at an Inter-faith seminary where every faith was embraced and welcomed. She embraced the truth at we are all children of God.

Her commitment to the mission of <u>Evangelical's Concerned</u> increased through the years, and in 2010 she felt led to run for a seat on the board. She was easily elected. When the new board members were introduced at the breakfast hour, I was thrilled for her and knew that her unique gifts, sensitivity and talents would make a good fit for the board.

After breakfast we walked to the first session where the founder, Dr. Ralph Blair was to speak. Eunice leaned over and said, "Be praying, I'm going to be called out by Dr. Blair."

I was shocked when a few minutes later he told of being blindsided by a board that would put an All-faith pastor into a board position with Evangelicals Concerned. He said that her inclusive acceptance of groups that worship God by other names was a personal offense to his standing in the Evangelical community.

My shock turned to anger when he stated he was not going to stand for her to be a board member. He further stated if need be, he would close down the thirty year ministry.

Eunice sat in stunned silence. She had no option other than to resign as a board member.

I was livid that Dr. Blair would publically draw a line in the sand from the pulpit. My view of inclusivity was impacted that day, but I vowed not to make public judgments on anyone's faith or personal choices.

It wasn't long before Evangelicals Concerned Western Region closed its doors after being an oasis of support for Gay Christians for almost thirty years. I believe the demise of this organization was due in part to the lack of inclusion of all people of faith.

As an African American Interfaith minister, and a woman, this was not the first time she had been on an opposing side of an issue of significance. She had dealt with her sexual orientation and her race issues for many years.

She had not yet confided her conflict with her gender identity. "I was a lesbian. I had a female body and that was all I knew about how to 'call' myself. I hung out with lesbians, and was attracted to women. However, something was missing. I just didn't feel complete as I embraced that identity."

On one of our many conversations since that time, I asked, "So, where are you on the journey now?" I listened to my own heart. *Don't make judgments, just listen.*

"I am a transgender male. I am heterosexual."

"And that is the reason for the name change I see on Facebook?"

"'Yes, I go by Yunus, which is Arabic for Jonah. Titles don't matter when it comes to loving. Everything is fluid in my life. I am a 56-year-old man regardless of my body. I have spent the last three years changing my pronouns. Gender and sexuality are not the same thing. At this point I don't think I will do the reassignment surgery. In my opinion it is not worth doing bottom surgery, for a number of reasons. It is expensive, and, in my opinion, it has not been perfected. I attended a Transgender conference in Philadelphia around mid-year 2013 and made the decision to embrace my true identity. I have been on hormone therapy since late 2013. I feel complete as a man."

I mentally scanned through the recent photos of his Facebook timeline. "And a handsome man you are Yunus. This has been a long journey for you."

She continued, "Over the last three years, I sought out many transgender persons and listened to their stories. I met a young woman, Male to Female and we talked for hours. That conversation led me to my truth. I am fully embracing the man I am, and identifying with the process."

"How does this impact your dating experiences?" I asked.

"I am dating a woman who is a lesbian, and now she is a lesbian who fell in love with a man." He paused. "We work it out. She affirms me as the man I am. I am not "out" at work and don't know when, if ever I will make the announcement. I look more masculine all the time, and I suppose eventually someone will ask. I know how devastating it would be if I lost my job. I am trying to establish my own business, so for the time being I am performing interfaith weddings and keeping a low profile. I have been receiving psychological counseling for several months and feel comfortable in my own skin."

So, I'm curious. "What about your family? Have you shared your transition with them?"

"Not at this point. My mom is elderly and is slowing down and I don't think it would be helpful to talk with her. My other family members do not live close by, so I don't have contact with them in person." He paused thoughtfully. "There is a lot of work to do for the Trans community. If I went underground, I couldn't be an advocate for transitioning and embracing the truth of who I am. I want to make myself known, and little by little, I am doing that. More specific legislation is needed in New York to help with reassignment surgery. I want to be part of that process.

"Well sir, you are looking good in your transition, and I'm honored to be your friend!" I paused. "Thank you for sharing the man you are with the world. I will continue to pray with you and support your efforts of making the world a safe place for all of God's children."

"Thank you. As yet another step in that direction, I was asked to be the East Coast Representative for the Fellowship of Affirming Ministries. I will be working with groups not only in the eastern states, but also with the national ministers. We have a big job with education and advocacy for all transgendered persons. I do appreciate your prayers."

CHAPTER 4

ROBIN AND MICHELLE
OUR JOURNEY INTO JOY

Psalm 30:11-12 *You turned my wailing into dancing; you removed my sackcloth and clothed me with joy, that my heart may sing to you and not be silent. O LORD my God, I will give you thanks forever.*

Picture this scene:

We're in our usual places, Robin at the counter and Michelle in the kitchen. Michelle is preparing a gourmet meal, and we are reviewing our lives as we wait for our friends—Gay, Straight, Lesbian and Trans—to arrive. God surely had a sense of humor when he put two female personalities into male bodies and sent them into the world to see what would happen. It has taken us fifty years to get the joke, but now our lives are filled with joy and laughter, good food and friends, wine and music. We wouldn't change our lives if we could!

ROBIN: I was born in 1957 in Sioux City, Iowa. My family was very religious, and I was involved in Sunday school and church from my earliest memories. I have two sisters, and always envied their comfort with their bodies because I was not comfortable with mine.

My family moved to California in 1961. I would spend hours fantasizing about being a girl. I was a good kid, and it never occurred to me to borrow my sisters' clothes. I did manage to collect some female clothes that I found, and dressed up in secret. I thought I was fairly normal. I was smart and I wasn't goofy looking, so I didn't understand why I didn't fit in with the other boys. Although I had heard stories of a couple of high profile transsexuals Christine Jorgenson and Renee Richards, I didn't understand that I was really a girl, or that the feelings I had made me just like them.

I remember being sad the day I realized that my voice was changing and I would no longer be able to sing in a pretty soprano voice. The first time my body reacted in a male way (while I was pretending to be a girl in the bath); I was very frightened and thought something was broken. I swore to God that I would never do that again if he would heal me. Of course, there was nothing for God to heal, I lived, and I continued to pretend to be a girl. I dressed up in private, and spent hours in my fantasy world.

During my school years, I would have one good friend at a time, with whom I would spend all my time. I didn't think of them as boyfriends. Looking back now, it seems obvious that this was a real emotional relationship, at least on my side. This was especially true with my high school friend Etienne. I remember becoming very jealous when he told me he had been out on a date with a girl.

My family was deeply involved in the Assembly of God church, and as was expected, after high school I enrolled in Southern California College with a major in Biblical Studies.

MICHELLE: I was born in 1959 in San Francisco, California. I was the middle child with older and younger sisters. From as early as I can remember, about age 3, I knew that I was really a girl. When my older sister Lynn went off to school I would put on one of her school dresses, and then go tell my parents "I'm going to go to school." For a while they thought it was cute, but then my dad became angry and told me "Boys don't wear dresses."

My family was Catholic, but we went to church irregularly, more often when my dad wasn't home. I went to catechism when I was about 8 or 9, and took my first Holy Communion.

At school, the boys would say I acted like a girl, and bullied me. I learned quickly that if I didn't want to hide in the library all day or get beat up, I had to hide behind a tough exterior. I could run real fast, and when the bullies followed me home, my ex-Green Beret father gave me the choice of fighting him or them, so I quickly learned to fight.

In my junior high school years, changes started happening in my body. Somehow I knew those changes would keep me from being the woman I always knew I was. I was depressed about this, and prayed to God to turn me into a girl. Every day I woke up and my body was more and more masculine.

Finally, in high school, I tried to forget about my gender conflicts. I became a long distance runner, and worked hard to maintain a good physical condition. By now I was able to win the fights, but I still couldn't get away from the knowledge that I was really a female. I continued to dress in my sisters' clothes at every opportunity. I shaped my eyebrows, and shaved my legs. Despite all this, I became a popular athlete, and girls found me attractive. I was also attracted to them, but I wanted to talk to them about clothes and such, not engage in romantic behavior. I never did talk about the clothes and makeup I wore in secret.

I moved on to Skyline Jr. College, which was mostly a continuation of my high school experiences. Then, I went to San Francisco State and majored in Physical Education. I was still running track and became an All-American athlete.

Girls would come to the track to watch me run and talk to me. One of them, Tiffany, stood out in the crowd. I instantly had a huge crush on her. I asked her out, and soon we were inseparable. About 3 months into our relationship she told me that I had the perfect face for makeup and did I mind if she put makeup on me?

I had to control my excitement, and told her to go ahead. As our relationship grew, it became an obsession for me to have her make me up. She thought it was fun, and liked to do it.

After college I accepted a commission in the United States Marine Corps. Tiffany and I were apart for about 3 months while I was in basic training school in Quantico Virginia. We couldn't bear to be apart, so I told her to meet me in Reno, and we would get married. On the day of our wedding I wore my dress white uniform and she wore a beautiful blue dress. We went to a wedding chapel and got married. When they pronounced us man and wife, I picked her up and carried her the four blocks to our honeymoon suite at a big hotel. She asked me not to wear makeup for that night, but I convinced her to put it on anyway.

In 1985, I left active duty and entered the United States Marine Corp Reserves. I needed a job, and became a dock supervisor on the swing shift in the freight industry. As the years passed, Tiffany became more and more frustrated with my cross-dressing. Now that I was working nights, she took the opportunity to start dating other men.

I eventually caught on, and we went to a marriage counselor who advised her that I would never change. The counselor didn't know much about what I was, however, she and Tiffany thought I should be exploring cross-dressing. When I caught Tiffany with another man and I knew our marriage was over, and I divorced her.

ROBIN: After graduation from college, I worked as the building manager for Christian Life Church, and I was self-employed as a handyman. I had grown up helping my dad fix things and figured what I didn't know, I could learn. I had lots of masculine skills to bolster my masculine persona.

On one job where I was hired to paint a bathroom for a tenant in an apartment complex. I met a woman who caught my attention. I began a short dating relationship with Justine. She was the first woman I really dated and was intimate with, but I wasn't ready for a sexual relationship. Our dating relationship didn't last long, although our friendship continued.

Then, in 1994, At the age of 37 I fell in love with a woman for the first time, and decided to get married. I hoped that being married would solve my desire to be a woman. Judy had 3 teenage daughters, and integrating my life with an instant family was quite a challenge, but I won the girls over, and became part of the family.

We found a house in downtown Long Beach that we liked. It was a 1911 Classical Revival duplex which needed a lot of work; however, at that price, I knew that I had all the skills to fix it. We bought it, and I began to work on upgrades. I was able to hide my true identity from Judy for 5 years, but eventually I started cross dressing again as I had in earlier years. I would sometimes dress in female clothes while I was working on empty apartments.

Then in 1999, disaster struck our make believe world. By now I was wearing panties under my clothes all the time. When I got undressed to go to bed, I would pull them down with my pants, except one day I forgot, so Judy saw what I was wearing and started asking me about it. I was forced to come out to her and reveal my life long obsession. She insisted I talk with our Pastor, Rob, who was less than sympathetic. I was forced to resign as an elder and give up my position on the trustee board.

Desperate to save our marriage, I attended counseling sessions with a therapist, Suzanne Ash, who tried to convince me that I was just a feminine man. That was no help. The girls were all out on their own by now, and Judy moved into her own apartment. She realized that if we were to remain married, she would end up in a lesbian relationship, which she was not prepared to do. We filed for divorce, although the process was not completed due to some legal technicalities.

It was about this same time that I started working for Benefit Programs Administration, which gave me a more stable income, and also is a much more typically feminine position, since about 80% of their workforce is female. Over the next couple of years I came out to my parents, siblings and stepchildren.

Our Pastor offered to have the church subsidize counseling with another therapist to see if my marriage could be salvaged. I found it difficult to talk to him, although the sessions did cause me to do a lot of thinking and reflection about who I was. I began experimenting with makeup and jewelry. I pierced my ears and finally got the courage to go out in public as myself. Mostly I went to movies, and was happy to be myself in public. The therapist was less than supportive of my feminine changes.

The first time I put my whole look together and looked at myself in the mirror; it was as if I was finally seeing the person who should have been there my whole life. I felt like mirrors had never worked correctly before. My family continued to try to convince me that I was in rebellion against God and was making a huge mistake. I met with my pastor several more times and he seemed genuinely to try to understand, but he simply could not get his mind around it. Meanwhile, I was finding more and more occasions to dress as myself.

MICHELLE: Shortly after divorcing Tiffany, I met Sheila at the freight office. I decided that I would never tell her about my dressing up. It was at this time that I also started exploring cross-dressing at a club called Powder Puffs of Orange County, and for the first time met other people like me. But, because I was with Sheila, I didn't give myself the chance to really find out who I was. I purged all my female clothes. I had grown out my fingernails, and the guys at work commented on them and joked among themselves that I had "girl nails". I didn't know it, but Sheila over heard these conversations, although she never mentioned it.

We got married in 1988. I tried really hard not to dress as a woman, although I occasionally borrowed her lipstick and make-up. My depression grew, and after about a year she confronted me about my depression, and about my long nails. I told her what I knew about myself. She was completely taken aback by this, but, she tried to be understanding. She let me dress up at home a couple of times, and she seemed to approve. I thought she was accepting me, but she became more and more disgusted with my dressing, and told me that she would divorce me if I dressed up again. I really wanted to stay with her so I purged my closet once again. However, my depression continued. In order to feel better about myself, I started to dress again knowing it would kill our relationship. Soon, we were living separate lives in the same house.

In 1996 I decided to leave my position with the Benefits department, to pursue the even manlier job of an LAPD officer. I was depressed and did not care whether I lived or died after I joined the force. I often volunteered for the most dangerous calls and quickly gained a reputation as a magnet for action.

I also excelled at learning the law, and began investigating robberies and major assault crimes. In 2002 I took the exam to become a detective and aced it. Because of my skills, I got the job of doing the very complex investigations for the LAPD Abused Child Unit. I received 34 commendations for my work with the LAPD.

In 2004 I could not stand the inner conflict of cross dressing to express my real identity, anymore. I had heard of a club called Tri-Es that was for straight men who were cross-dressers. Transsexuals were not allowed, but I was in denial about what I really was. The meetings were at a hotel one weekend a month and I told Sheila that I really needed to do this. She begrudgingly allowed me to attend, but we grew farther apart emotionally.

Finally, at one meeting in 2005 a woman named Leigh, who did laser hair removal, came to one of the meetings and gave demonstrations. Because my beard was thick and dark, I decided to have it removed. Leigh and I had a connection. She was good looking and interested in me, and also knew about my feminine side, so it seemed like I might have a chance at a life with her.

She left her partner, and after a long period of contemplation I decided to divorce Sheila and marry Leigh. Then things changed. Once we had built a relationship she told me she didn't want me to dress up anymore.

I was committed to the relationship and once again I tried to comply with her request. Once again, I struggled with deep depression. Then, I found out she was an alcoholic, and that she also did drugs. She introduced me to crystal meth. The rush made me feel happy and I was able to forget about my problems for a little while. But, I still wanted to be a woman and I did not care if I died. I actually prayed to God to let me die so I could be reincarnated as a girl. I overdosed on cocaine and ended up in the hospital, where they reported the incident to the LAPD. I loved being a detective with the LAPD, but with that on my record, I was forced to resign in 2007.

I moved back to my quiet Orange County neighborhood and went back to work for Conway Trucking. I divorced Leigh in 2008.

ROBIN: In 2006 Judy decided she wanted to cash out her share of our home, since we had been separated several years, so we sold it. I felt I was reaching the point of a decision of whether to transition or not when Justine, a woman I previously dated came back into my life after 10 years of no contact. She convinced me that this transition was against God's will, and I should purge my home of all things feminine and seriously try to live as a man. I had purged before, but this time was a real sacrifice, because I had actually spent a lot of money buying clothes, shoes, jewelry and makeup. I felt I was doing it for God. Nevertheless, despite my best intentions, nothing felt different.

The best result that came from this experience is that I became convinced that God had created me just the way I am! I realized also that I could never change the fact that I was a girl, and that I must embrace my true gender identity. It occurred to me that God would have to admit that He made a mistake if He answered my prayers and changed the way He had made me! I started rebuilding my wardrobe, wig and makeup collection

It was 2010 when I was able to obtain hormones without a prescription. I started using Rogaine to fill in my bald spot, and decided it was time to find a counselor that I could work with, and be honest about who I was, and talk about my determination to transition.

In October 2010, Dr. Christine Milrod and I had our first session. I was immediately comfortable with her. By this time, I was going as myself everywhere except t work and church. I debated meeting her in male mode, but then I thought, why should I?

Her first words to me were "Oh, you're already female." I was able to share openly and honestly about myself for the first time in my life.

Pastor Rob had told me that if I came to church as myself, I "would be upstaging God." I thought his God must be small if I could upstage him, so I decided to find another church where I would be accepted as I transitioned.

I visited <u>Glory Tabernacle Christian Center</u> in Long Beach. I was familiar with the worship music and the pastor, Rev. Sandra Turnbull had been raised in an Assembly of God church, so I felt comfortable with her spiritual background. She is a lesbian who has been through her own struggles to come out to her family. My heart was very touched with the message and I felt very much at home.

I was in tears as I stood in my pleated black skirt and frilly purple top, while we sang over and over, "Oh How He Loves Us." I decided that I would leave my old church right after the New Year. Every time I had a session with Christine, I would rave about how amazing my new church was, and how loving and accepting the people were.

I play the violin, and had played with a Christian orchestra based in Orange County, *The Praise Symphony Orchestra*, for 27 years. I was eager to transition, and I hoped that I could remain with them. On a Monday night, I wrote a letter to the director and board, and left it on the director's stand after practice. The director called Tuesday, and asked if she and a couple of board members could speak with me. They came to my house on Wednesday. After a short conversation, they informed me that I was not welcome among them, effective immediately.

I had a violin that belonged to the orchestra and the keys to their equipment van, so I gave them both back, and that's the last I heard from any of them, except for my stand partner, who expressed her regret at the way I was treated.

Dr. Christine Milrod follows the World Professional Association of Transgender Health standards of care very closely—12 sessions of therapy and 1 session with a consulting psychiatrist before writing a letter recommending hormone replacement therapy by a physician. I was still several months away from the point where she would recommend for me to begin HRT, but I was able to obtain more hormones without a prescription. I did tell her what I was doing, though.

It was on the first Sunday of 2011, I officially joined Glory Tabernacle. It was also about this time that I began electrolysis to get rid of my beard. I had worn a beard most of my adult life as protection against going out in public as a woman. When I finally shaved it and started going out as myself, it was a big turning point. By that time my beard had started to turn white, so I was not a good candidate for laser treatment. I found an electrologist not too far from my home and began the weekly torture sessions.

One of Christine's homework assignments was to try going out to some social events with other transgendered people. One Tuesday I went to a T-girl night at Hamburger Mary's. It really wasn't my thing, and I sat in a corner drinking a soda by myself. A man came over and asked if he could join me. He was a ruggedly handsome older man. We talked as well as we could over the loud music.

He asked if he could see me again and gave me his card. Before we left, he kissed me, which I liked very much. I started dating Bannister whenever he was in town. He lived in Washington D.C, but came to Los Angeles often on business. He treated me like a lady, and I liked being with him. He was a fascinating guy who had always been attracted to transgendered women.

About that time, Christine connected me with a couple of her clients who were also transitioning. In February 2011 Michelle and I met at a Starbucks before church. We connected immediately, and began to share our stories. Then she came to a church service which was unlike anything she had been to in her Catholic church. She wasn't scared away. We met the next Sunday, and went out to lunch after church, and continued to share our experiences with each other.

MICHELLE: In December 2010, I hit my rock bottom. I was at a Christmas party, and two beautiful women were flirting with me. I knew I could have taken either one of them to bed with me that night. Then I saw it happen all over again: I was going to fall in love and get married. Then she would find out who I really was and we would get divorced. My life seemed to be going in circles. I was depressed and thought that I could never transition, so I determined to end it all. I didn't want to ruin the holiday season for my family, so I put my affairs in order.

Then in January, I was sitting on my couch, drinking Scotch, cleaning my nine-millimeter, and getting ready to end my life, when I heard a voice in my head say "You've never gotten help for this; you can always kill yourself later." I got on line and searched for Transgender Therapists and made an appointment with Dr. Christine Milrod. For the next two weeks I kept thinking I wouldn't actually go to see her. I was going to cancel, but I thought, "She doesn't have anything but my email; she can't charge me for a missed appointment."

The day of the appointment arrived, and I wasn't going to go, but the little voice said, "You might as well see where her office is, you don't have to go in." Then, "you might as well take a look inside, you can always leave." As I entered the waiting room, Christine stepped out of her office and asked "Michelle?" I went into her office, and for the first time in my life told someone else all the things that were going on in my head.

In our first session the subject of church came up and she asked me if I liked attending that church. I said I went sometimes, and she told me she had someone she wanted me to meet. I gave her permission to give Robin my contact information. We met before church the next Sunday and made an immediate connection.

The Glory Tab was so different from the Catholic churches I had occasionally attended. I wasn't sure they were for real, but everyone was so friendly and welcoming. The worship music was amazing, and it seemed like Pastor Sandy was preaching directly to me. I heard about a God who cared about me, personally, and with whom I could have a relationship. God loves me just as I am, and had in fact created me just the way I was. I started praying, and meditating on what I was learning, and God spoke to my heart and helped me understand all the ways I had harmed others throughout my life. I asked for his forgiveness and the strength to live my life in his ways, and began to experience the peace I had longed for all my life. *God really loves me. He didn't make a mistake!*

ROBIN: I spent every Sunday with Michelle. We had so much in common and I began to care deeply for her. She was easy to be with, and I could relate to her stories. I moved forward with my divorce from Judy. I decided to speak with my boss at Benefits Program Administration regarding my transition. The company determined that I should wait until I had my new identity documents showing my gender as female before I transitioned at work, and I agreed to that.

In April 2011, I completed my 12th session with Christine. I was feeling really good about my appearance, and my hair had grown in enough that I no longer needed my wig. I also began my hormone injections that month.

I took my first legal step in transition when I filed for a name change with the courts. My first name, "Robin" can go either way, and I had always thought of it as female, so I didn't change that. I selected "Celeste" as my new middle name, which I thought was beautiful, and had the advantage of starting with the same letter and was the same length as the old name that I hated. The same day my court ordered name change came through, I contacted Social Security and DMV to get my identity documents. As far as the state is concerned, I was legally female!

At that time, the DMV required a form signed by a doctor certifying irreversible treatment (HRT qualifies) to change gender on your identity documents. Social Security required a surgeon's letter that was for the name change only, not gender. The gender change with Social Security had to wait until after my surgery.

MICHELLE: I started hormones on May 9th 2011. Robin and I were spending every weekend together. We attended the Gay Pride Parade in Long Beach with Glory Tabernacle, and we carried the church's banner. It was a special time of bonding.

Robin and I planned a week-long trip to San Francisco as ourselves for the middle of June 2011. This was the first outing of our transition on a 24/7, no turning back basis. As part of our trip preparation, I went with Robin as she had her first "girl" haircut. While I was waiting, I talked to the manicurist at the shop, and we both came back later that day and had our nails done by Naomi. The trip was partly a test to see how we would get along together for an extended period of time, and we enjoyed every minute. On the way north, I remarked to Robin that I wasn't ready to call myself a "born-again Christian" yet, but I was really enjoying our church. She read Romans 10:10 to me and told me she knew that I believed in Christ because I had been brought up Catholic, and now I was telling everyone I could about what God was doing for me, so I was actually the definition of born again! I was surprised, but happy. Our week together ended all too soon. Robin was going back to work as herself, but I would have to endure going back to work in male mode. I kept my nails on until the last possible moment!

ROBIN: June 6, 2011 was the first day of going to work as myself! I had been sharing about my transition with the other four women in the office all along, and they were very supportive. Unfortunately, some women from another suite in the building complained about me using the women's restroom. Although I had every legal right and could have fought it, I agreed to use a unisex handicapped restroom on the floor below. That embarrassed me, and I tried to time my visits so no-one would wonder why I was using that room instead of the regular restroom. In fact, the women on that floor would hold the door for me if I happened to be approaching the restroom at the same time as they were, and chatted with me, so I knew they completely accepted me, unlike the women in the suite next to us.

Michelle and I started talking about becoming room-mates. Transition is expensive, even for people with fulltime jobs, so this seemed like a good thing to do, besides the fact that I was already spending all my time at her house.

MICHELLE: I had a 3-5-year plan for my transition process. That way, I wouldn't have to come out to my family or work for at least a couple of years. However, God and my therapist were moving me along faster than I had thought possible. I was a little envious, because Robin could use her checks and credit cards from the beginning since her birth name could go either way. I avoided using credit cards and hated to have to show sales clerks my old driver's license. In June I was finally able to file for my name change.

My mother had told me that if I had been born a girl she would have named me "Michelle" so I had always thought of that as my real name. Robin helped me choose my new middle name, "Renee", which means "re-born." I was very happy when I got my name change order from the court, and then the same day my new driver's license and Social Security card.

That brought up a new problem though. All my identity documents said I was Michelle Skiff, female, but my work didn't have any idea yet. The freight industry is a very male-dominated, macho environment, and I was terrified about what I thought might happen when I told them who I really was. I was still going to work in male-mode, and one night, a driver who I had known for many years said to me, "What the F***? You look like a girl!"

I was scared, and texted Robin, and emailed Christine, but God was starting to make things uncomfortable for me and I would have to come out at work soon.

Telling Patrick, my 6'4" Texan boss that I was really a girl was one of the most terrifying things I have done in my life. I would have rather broken down the door of a crack house filled with armed gangsters! I wrote him a letter, then made an appointment with him, and read it. I couldn't believe his reaction. His biggest fear was that I was going to tell him I was quitting my job.

He suggested I contact the company's regional head of Human Relations to plan my transition. The HR director told me I was the first transsexual to transition at Conway, and I was therefore the *de-facto* subject matter expert. We decided that I would first meet on October 1st with my shift supervisors to let them know what was going to happen, and then come out to the whole company.

Starting with my regular night shift on October 3, and continuing on through the next day, I met with each shift and introduced them to Michelle. I briefly told them my story, and took questions. I was expecting resistance and disbelief. When I first came into the meetings, there was some laughter, and a few people thought it was a joke. However, after I shared my story, almost everyone expressed their support.

Diana, who I had known for many years, was in tears, and my good friend Jammer told me he had never suspected, but he was happy for me. Only one person out of the over 200 that I came out to, reacted the way I had expected. That same night an email went out to all the company's management people throughout the country announcing the change, so I came out to over 2,000 people in one night.

Robin and I moved ahead with combining our two households, and in October she moved in with me, as roommates. Robin also finalized her divorce with Judy on November 2.

We marveled at the parallel events in our lives that brought us to this place in our transition. Surly God had directed our paths, because the chances that we would ever have met were so remote and next to impossible. In the events that followed, we were finding ourselves more together than separate. While we had a growing attraction to one another, there was a reluctance to move forward in our relationship. We both felt like we were experiencing the best friendship we had ever had in our lives and worried about what might happen if our relationship became more intimate. The big question is what would happen if things didn't work out?

We spent our first holidays together and had monthly sessions with Christine to satisfy WPATH guidelines. Those guidelines mandated 12 additional sessions and another session with a consulting psychiatrist for the letter recommending surgery. It was obvious to our therapist and just about everyone else who knew us that we were in love. We continued to resist the idea.

Then on a rainy Sunday afternoon in March, we had a fire in the fireplace, listening and dancing to country music, and we ended up kissing each other. A few minutes later I was in the kitchen and Robin was sitting at the counter, and we started talking. We both shared our fears about what could happen, but we came to the conclusion that we had lived our lives long enough in fear and hiding. We didn't want to make that mistake again. Our new lives together would be based on love and truth. We admitted to ourselves and our friends that we were more than just friends, we were now a couple.

ROBIN: I had expected that any future relationships would be with a woman, and I was more surprised that I could be attracted to a man as I was with Banister from the T-Bar. My therapist assured me that it was not uncommon for transsexuals to be somewhat bisexual. However, I had not had to consider myself homosexual before, since I had been living as a man with Judy, and then seeing Banister, as a woman. Now it was indisputable. I was in love with another woman who was exactly like me. No matter how we sliced it, we were in a same sex relationship.

In college, I had read, *Is the Homosexual My Neighbor?* by Scanzoni & Mollencott. More recently in my previous church I had met gay couples who were good Christian people. I also had met many loving, Christian friends at Glory Tab. But that was THEM…now it's ME! I had to go through all "those" scriptures again. But once again I came to the same conclusion…the behaviors the Bible condemns as an abomination have to do with the worship of false gods and idols, and not with homosexuality *per se.*

MICHELLE: We had a lot of first experiences. In February 2012, we celebrated our first friendship anniversary with breakfast at Schooner or Later, a popular little restaurant in the Long Beach

Marina. This was also the first I went out in public "organic", no wig, no breast forms. In March we shared our first kiss. Then at a Gay Pride planning meeting we announced to our church family that we were lesbians, and officially a "couple". The reactions ranged from applause, to jaw dropping expressions, and one friend fell off her chair. We were happier than we had ever been in our lives.

ROBIN: There are some who were not accepting of our transition or our union of hearts. My parents continue to disapprove of me, and will not see Michelle. My sisters have both been in our home, although they have a lot of reservations about our relationship.

I had always thought that Michelle had a beautiful face, but she thought her nose was too big. She underwent Facial Feminization surgery in May. It was out-patient surgery and my first nerve-wracking wait while she went under the knife.

We both began what Michelle calls "Australian" electrolysis, which is preparation "down under" for Gender Reassignment Surgery. The hair on the skin that will be used to create a vagina has to be cleared, which takes about a dozen sessions of an hour each. Naturally this is a rather personal and potentially embarrassing procedure, but our electrologist Layla makes her clients feel at ease during this uncomfortable and painful experience.

In September 2012, we made a trip over Labor Day to Reno, Nevada to visit with Michelle's parents. They had already been to our home a couple of times and accepted me very well. They were also very accepting of Michelle, although they still had some trouble getting used to using her right name. We hadn't told them yet about our new relationship. When we arrived at their house, they had an air bed set up, as well as a pull-out couch. But Michelle's

Mom took her aside right away and asked about us. Michelle told them we were officially a couple, and gave them a picture of us that she had brought along. They were genuinely pleased for us, and Mom immediately put the airbed away. A few days later, we headed back to California.

I put my house in Long Beach on the market and it sold quickly, generating enough cash to pay for my Gender Reassignment surgery. With exactly enough money in my bank account, I called Dr. Bowers' office to make an appointment for my surgery. I was hoping for early 2013 but the next available opening was in September 2013. That was eleven long months away.

Michelle's appointment had been scheduled only 4 months after she contacted them and my hopes for a date in the spring were quickly dashed to pieces. We celebrated the Thanksgiving holiday with much for which to be thankful, even though I managed to break the oven the night before our fabulous dinner! Fortunately, we have two ovens, but I had to text Michelle and tell her that I broke the one, so she would have to do all her cooking with only one oven. We made it an event to remember with several friends from church.

MICHELLE: My Gender Reassignment Surgery was set for December 5, 2012. Robin and I traveled to San Francisco to meet with Dr. Marci Bowers at Peninsula Hospital in Burlingame, California. Dr. Bowers is one of the outstanding experts in the field of reassignment surgery, who happens to be one of *us*. Her clients come from all over the country and around the world. She is also a caring and personable doctor. The hospital was beautiful, clean and new. Dr. Bowers has a suite of 6 rooms for her patients, and the staff to care for each of her patients. They are all very considerate and friendly.

I had elected to have breast augmentation in conjunction with my GRS, which saves a lot of money on that procedure, since you are already in the operating room and the surgical staff is assembled. The majority of the extra cost is for the cosmetic surgeon. The extra hospital costs are minimal and it also saves on recovery time.

On Monday, I met with Dr. Bowers and also the cosmetic surgeon Dr. Joel Beck for final consultations. I picked up my prescriptions, including the "human draino" that I would be taking the next day to clean out my body in preparation for the surgery. My friend and running partner from college days, Mike Gulli, visited with me for several hours on Tuesday while I was waiting for the anxiety to lessen about my surgery. This was the first time I had seen him in years. That evening was spent laughing and talking with Debbie, a woman who had just been through her surgery and was almost ready to go home, along with her wife Birgitta.

I spent a restless night before the surgery with thoughts spinning wildly through my mind. Wednesday morning finally arrived and Robin and I arrived in plenty of time. They started prepping me for surgery almost immediately. Dr. Bowers usually does two surgeries on the days she operates I was scheduled for the second surgery of the morning, starting about 11:30. Robin was able to be with me until they were ready to take me in to the operating room. We talked and prayed together. I was at peace.

ROBIN: Once the hallway doors closed and Michelle was out of sight, I had a long wait ahead of me. I knew that I wouldn't possibly hear anything until at least 3:30. So after a while I couldn't stand waiting any longer and went shopping!

I got back to the hospital around 3:00, and finally around 4:00 Dr. Bowers came out and told me that Michelle had done very well.

Now it was Dr. Beck's turn, and his procedure was done around 5:30. They told me Michelle would be in recovery until about 7:00. I was hungry, and I wanted to get her some flowers, so I went out. When I got back to the hospital at 6:30, Michelle was already in her room. The nurses told me that in the recovery room, while she was waking up, she had repeatedly asked them "where is Robin?"

MICHELLE: When I woke up, I knew that I was finally myself. The person I had tried to suppress for all those years was finally a reality. As groggy as I was, I picked up my phone and announced on Facebook, "I'm alive and I'm me! Talk to you all tomorrow."

ROBIN: The rooms at Peninsula Hospital have an alcove in the window area that can be made into a bed for a patient's partner, so I was able to stay with Michelle the entire time, except for trips back to the hotel room to shower and change my clothes.

On Thursday Dr. Bowers came in to check on Michelle, and to change her bandages. I got to see the results. I had never seen "down there" before, as we were always careful of respecting that area of privacy with each other, I knew what had been there, and it took me back a bit. I thought to myself, "Do you really want to have that done to yourself?" And about a half-second later, came the answer, "Damn straight I do!"

On Friday the nurses got Michelle out of bed, and we made a couple of circuits around the ward. Dana joined us in our excursions. She had been a pilot in the Air Force, so she and Michelle had a connection with their military experience. Michelle made us laugh with a rendition of what a drill sergeant in the Marines would be saying to transsexual recruits. After all, the military has procedures for everything! Another friend from high school days came and visited Michelle for a couple of hours in the hospital.

Michelle was discharged around noon on Saturday, and I drove her back to the hotel, where I spent the next couple of days taking care of her, following Dr. Bowers' recommendation that her patients stay nearby for 10 days, in case of complications. There were none, and by the following Friday Michelle wanted to go home, so we packed up the car and headed back to southern California.

MICHELLE: In February 2013, we celebrated our 2nd year of friendship at Schooner or Later again. In April I went back to court for the last time to complete my legal gender change. The court order came back in June, and then I had to send it to the California State Registrar to have a new birth certificate issued. It seemed like an afterthought to me when my new birth certificate arrived, stating that Michelle Renee Skiff had been born female. I was finished with transitioning and just wanted to get on with my life.

Neither of us proposed to the other, but we just naturally started talking about getting married. We started making plans, thinking about all the details that had been left up to our fiancées for our previous weddings. We looked at pictures of wedding dresses, chose our colors. We looked at bouquet designs, and thought about our vows. That summer, we began preparations for our wedding, which would take place in August at Glory Tabernacle, and Rev. Sandy Turnbull would officiate the first Lesbian wedding at the new church building.

Since Robin hadn't had her surgery yet, we figured that if same sex marriages were not yet re-instated in California, she could use her passport, which still indicated her gender as male, as her ID to get our license. Fortunately, in June Proposition 8 was struck down, and we were able to get a marriage license with our correct genders. The day we got our license, there were 2 other gay couples who also applied for a license. One of the lesbian couples from Arizona was celebrating their anniversary by getting legally married. There were several heterosexual couples, including an interracial couple. Michelle remarked that if that collection of people had shown up to get marriage licenses 30 years ago, there probably would have been a riot!

THE WEDDING.
August 11 finally arrived. While our friends from church made all the preparations, transforming the sanctuary for our wedding, we were getting ready for our big day. Michelle and her team were at the house, and Robin and her team were at the hotel where we would spend our wedding night. The white wedding dresses that were exactly what we had always imagined, and with hair and make-up done, we made our way to the church in separate vehicles. Both of us wore white gowns. After all we were special kinds of virgins on this most holy day.

Most of our church family was there, along with friends from work. Michelle's mom & step-father were escorted down the aisle, and lit the unity candles. Then Robin's Matron of Honor came down the aisle, followed by Robin, who was escorted by our friend Chris. Next were Michelle's Matron of Honor, and finally Michelle, escorted by our friend Paul. Standing side by side in our white gowns, our blond hair was adorned with flower head pieces that supported white lace veils. The lace veil arch under which we stood framed us perfectly.

We could hardly contain our emotions. With tears streaming down our cheeks, we looked into each other's eyes and recited the vows that we had written. It was a blessed day. We were both happier than we thought was possible. The rest of the day went by in a blur of toasts, cutting the cake and dancing. It was not just pretend dress up, and all our years of longing to be ourselves were finally realized.

ROBIN: One month later, we were on our way to San Francisco for my Gender Reassignment Surgery, also with Dr. Bowers. I had been with Michelle when she went through her surgery, so I knew what to expect. I had the same slot in Dr. Bowers' weekly schedule, so the events happened on the same days of the week.

When Michelle and I arrived at the Hospital, Michelle got to stay with me during the preparations, and we talked and prayed. At last we were ready. They wheeled me down the hallway and I said goodbye to Michelle. A couple of twists and turns and hallways later, they brought me into a room that looked like it belonged in a spaceship. Everything was gleaming white, and all sorts of equipment was suspended from the ceiling. About the only thing that looked familiar besides the gurney I was on was the huge vital statistics monitor on the wall. I had about a minute to look around as they started to work on me, and then I was out.

From the patient's point of view, surgery is a piece of cake. One second you are getting ready for the surgery and the next you are opening your eyes and waking up in a recovery room. What is hard is for your loved one who has to experience those 5 long hours of anxious waiting. I woke up in my room, happy and satisfied that I would never have to look in the mirror again and see a body that didn't match my mental image of myself.

The pain level was very manageable, except the next day when the nurses tried to turn me to change my bedding. I had also elected to have breast augmentation at the same time as my GRS, so when they turned me to the side, the pain level in my chest shot up to about 10. I could move forward and back ok, but not to the side! Michelle stayed with me in the room, and the next couple of days were a blur.

The hospital staff does not usually see their charges again after they leave the hospital, so it was a special treat for them to see Michelle nine months later, healed up and doing well. They all remembered us from our first trip, and were happy for us getting married. They enjoyed the wedding pictures we shared with them.

On Friday the nurses got me up, and I walked around the ward a couple of times, and by noon on Saturday I was ready to go back to the hotel. You remain on a catheter for the first six days, so ironically, you find yourself standing up to pee (to empty the bag) after it's no longer possible to do so. Michelle's drill sergeant persona had had some choice things to say about this during her recovery.

The next few days Michelle took care of me, while I got stronger and was able to be up and about for longer periods of time. On Tuesday, I went to Dr. Bowers' office to have the catheter removed. Then on the next day we celebrated Michelle's birthday by going into the city and having lunch at a nice restaurant. We drove back home on Friday. Then I spent another 2 weeks at home recovering before returning to work.

Michelle's legal gender change with the state of California was a continuation of her name-change filing. Since I was born in Iowa, I had to contact the Iowa Department of Health. Their process turned out to be very simple. They sent me a form which I had to fill out, along with the letter from my surgeon, my name change order, and $20. A few weeks later, in November, I had an

Iowa birth certificate in my hands that declared that Robin Celeste Stearns had been born female...the truth at last.

December 2013 was our first holiday as a legally married couple. We are blessed to share our love for God and for each other, and we are enjoying life as God intended for us. We thank God every day for the love he has given us and the life he has put before us. We pray that God will use us in service to himself and others.

CHAPTER 5

"JULIE"
MALE TO FEMALE
FROM CONVENT TO COMPASSION

I spent years hiding in plain sight. I didn't reveal anything about my transition to the Superior Mother when I applied for entrance to the convent and, thankfully, it never came up during my time there. I was able blend in and just be part of this community of women and remain as one of their own.

I was respected and loved for the gifts I brought to the Community, and they made good use of my talents.'

During my time in religious life, I had the opportunity to meet some truly remarkable, amazing women from a number of religious orders. They were well educated, articulate, and had a good grasp of social issues and causes promoting peace and justice.

I loved these women, and I learned so much from them that continues to factor into my daily life. Sisters, historically, were the ones "in the trenches," so to speak. The clergy resided in their well-appointed rectories, seminaries, and bishop residences. The

Sisters, on the other hand, were often left in housing that was sorely inadequate; lacked heating, suitable furniture, and even a lack of food was not at all uncommon.

Sisters and Nuns have always been the unsung heroines of the Church, and, consequently, were never compensated for their years of dedicated service. Many of them are totally dependent on the Community to care for them in their golden years because the Church never set anything aside to assist them in their old age. Male clergy, on the other hand, usually enjoy handsome retirement benefits.

By the way, there is a distinction between nuns and sisters, although people use the two interchangeably. The difference is in the type of vows professed. Sisters take simple vows, while Nuns profess solemn vows.

These women are the backbone and lifeblood of the church; they feed and clothe the poor, they nurse the sick, and they make sure the children receive a quality education.

Because of their close connection working hands-on with the people, they had marvelous insight into the struggles and complexities of human life, and the wisdom they shared through their combined experiences taught me much about the absolute necessity for unconditional love and compassion to ALL of God's people.

Their apostolates of devotion and service brought them face to face with the issue facing the LGBT community, and many of these women are among our strongest allies because they understand and live, through the example of their own lives, the commandment of love.

During my time with them I witnessed firsthand the beauty of self-sacrifice, the offering of oneself to God that He might use us as His instrument to reach those who needed Him most. It was an incredibly spiritual experience for me, and I will never forget how it transformed my life and my perspective.

However, long before that transformation, my life was hell. My mother had always wanted a girl, and I desperately wanted to be a girl. I knew at the very core of me, Julie was alive and well. On the outside, I was tormented and bullied all through my school years in the 1960's. I was different. I just didn't understand my "identity" at all.

One poignant memory from my childhood was after the birth of my sister. I had a stroller and my dolls which I took on daily walks in the neighborhood, much to the horror of the neighbors who were very concerned that Kim was being raised a queer and therefore I was not allowed to play with other children for fear that they would catch my disease. I was no longer permitted to dress girly.

My father was very disgusted with my mother and personally took me to the barber who shaved off my long beautiful curls, and forced me to burn all the girl toys I had. I can still remember having to throw my dolls and doll buggy in the fire. I cried buckets of tears for days over that. I do still have my Mickey Mouse doll. My mom managed to save him from the burning barrel, and my dad allowed me to keep him.

My dolls were destroyed; however, Julie was alive and well inside Kim's body. I was on the path to setting her free and embracing all that she would become. Trans folks were not well accepted, and I knew that I didn't identify as Gay.

When I was in High School, I confessed my feelings to a friend, by trying to explain my confusion.

She told me I was probably gay, and needed to pursue a relationship with another gay man. I wanted to go to the Junior prom as a girl, which is what I felt in my heart. I was prevented from doing that by my mom, who was not at all understanding or sympathetic to my internal conflicts.

Just before the prom, I was attacked by a group of boys in the locker room, and was gang raped. Everyone sat around and watched, jeering and encouraging the attack. No one came to my defense or called security for help. When they finally allowed me to leave, I rushed home to tell my mother of the attack.

She was not sympathetic at all, and in fact told me I must have done something to invite the attack, and it was my entire fault. My parents were divorced at this time, so my dad didn't have any input into the situation.

I was emotionally destroyed and despondent for weeks. I finally decided to commit suicide. I left a "good-bye" note, and told my one girl friend what I was going to do. I had stored up enough pills to accomplish the job, and felt the world would be better off without me. I only had one adult friend at school, a teacher who happened also to be gay. I was afraid to actually talk with him because I knew the school was trying to get him fired. I decided to just take the pills, and die.

This was another thing I couldn't do successfully. My girlfriend was afraid for me and called the police. They showed up at my home, and rushed me off to the hospital, where they pumped my stomach. My mom was brought to the hospital, and she was livid that I had created a scene with the police. I was once again left on my own to deal with my depression and my failure to even kill myself.

I was released to my mom's care, and was told that we would be hearing from the school authorities and from the court system. My mom worried more that I was an embarrassment to her, rather than trying to help me adjust to my own struggle.

Within days, we appeared in court, and I was ordered not to return to school. In fact, I was banned from the Tacoma school grounds and would have to be tutored at home if I planned to graduate. My mom and I were in daily conflicts about my emotional state, and she finally called the authorities to say I had threatened her. It was just an excuse to have me removed from the home. I never threatened her with physical harm. My name was "Kim" at the time and they treated me as a hostile teenage boy.

The police came and took me to juvenile hall for threatening her. I was locked up wearing only a pair of gym shorts, socks and a tee shirt. I spent four days in solitary confinement!

Although my parents were divorced, my dad did come to visit me. Due to the complications of their custody agreement, he was blocked from making any changes to help me gain release. My mom wanted me committed to Western Washington State Hospital, but Dad would not sign the consent forms. Mom didn't want me to come back home.

In 1973, when I had just turned seventeen, and was getting back on track with completing classes to graduate, the school called and said I needed to come down to the school and discuss an "issue" in person. I couldn't figure out what could be wrong, so I went, expecting a discussion about my classes. At this point, I was still doing independent study at home.

I was met by the police who took me to a room for interrogation.

The cop was stern. "A crime has been committed and you are an accessory."

"I haven't been involved in any crime," I insisted. I didn't know at the time, that my mother had gone to the school to report that the "gay" teacher had had sex with me. She had it in her mind that I was a sexual pervert and was convinced that something had occurred with him. The police kept me in the room for several hours trying to get me to confess to having a sexual involvement with Mr. Gaylord. Their tactics were sheer intimidation. However, I kept insisting it did not happen.

The school district fired Mr. Gaylord from the school, and filed charges against him for child abuse. I was compelled to attend the court proceedings, and continued to deny that anything had happened with him.

Even though I denied any sexual involvement with Mr. Gaylord, my mother still believed I was perverted. She knew about my experience with the gang rape with boys my own age I was sure that I was not gay, and when I was 18, I began to take hormones to transition to my feminine self. In the early 1970's there was not a lot of information or support for transgendered youth. I was determined to make a way, even without my mother's support. She was also involved with the Baptist church, and was soliciting advice from them as to how to deal with my rebellion.

Soon after I had begun transition my mother became aware of it and not long she contacted a Christian ministry and support group for mothers of children who are LGBT. Spatula Ministries was founded by a woman named Barbara Johnson, when her own son came out as gay. I believe that message of this ministry was to preach about the sin of homosexuality and encourage mothers to pray their children out of it. However, in the end, Mrs. Johnson was resolved to love her son as he was, and the ministry went out of business.

My mother was very involved in all of this, and it was through Barbara Johnson's ministry she became a devout follower of Perry Desmond. He was a former trans person who was allegedly delivered by God from his sin of transsexualism. He went on to become a "Eunuch for the Lord," joining forces with many notable Christian personalities. He was also exploited by many big name televangelists, and he used to tour with Pat Boone.

Within weeks, I started to receive mail from Perry Desmond telling me that he was praying for my deliverance from the devil and a life of perversion and sin. My mother even paid to fly Perry to Washington state so that she could bring him to my home. I had recently moved, in order to have privacy, and not be harassed. She was convinced that if he "laid hands on me" I would be delivered from this sin.

I was not there when they came, but my housemate at the time told me that they forced their way into the house. Together, they went through all my clothes, make-up and other personal items, praying that Satan would be evicted and I would be saved. I was absolutely furious when I found out.

They returned another day to host a prayer meeting in my front yard with other "Christians" to pray that the evil would be exorcised from the house and me. I was not there when that happened either, but the neighbors got quite a show.

My mother told me numerous times that I was an evil perfume in the sight of the Lord and that He would spit me from His mouth into everlasting hell, where I would burn for all eternity unless I repented of my sin. She said I needed to give my life to the Lord, and live the life of the man He created me to be.

My mother proclaimed herself to be God's apostle for delivering transgendered people from their sin. She found her way on to the Christian TV station in Aberdeen, where she hosted a children's program for a few years called, <u>God's Hurray Gang</u>.

Perry Desmond eventually died from complications relating to the huge amounts of silicone he had injected during the course of his transition. I am thankful that the ministry died with him.

Sadly, there are many men and women who have slipped through the psychological cracks and entered transition therapy. They are not truly Trans and have then come back to condemn the rest of us. The gender programs are quite good at weeding out those who are not suitable for this therapy, but those who make it through and then fail because they had other greater life issues become some of the worst opponents to transitioning.

But this doesn't mean that the rest of us are on the wrong path and will also fail to live our authentic lives. The statistics are quite clear that there are a significantly decreased number of suicides among those who find appropriate services and are able to transition successfully.

Our opponents would have us believe otherwise, but having lived through it, I know firsthand this is true. The suicide rate it is directly proportionate to the persecution, rejection and abuse we suffer from those who cannot and will not demonstrate compassion, caring, and kindness. Unfortunately, far too many Christians have a great deal to learn about God's commandment to "love one another," which includes their transgendered brothers and sisters.

During the course of all of my transition, my mother went out of her way to proclaim my "sin" to anyone who would listen. When confronted about exposing the private details of my life to everyone, she told me that it was her duty as a Christian and a mother to proclaim my sin before all, because I was deceiving the most holy God.

The only remedy she saw as a mother suffering from the sinful nature of her child was to do what she felt the Holy Spirit told her to, and that was to proclaim my sin to the nations. At one point she contacted TBN in an effort to have Paul and Jan Crouch hear her story of the "innocent Christian mother who was being martyred by a son who was caught in the throes of sin and perversion." My mother always had a great flair for the melodramatic and thrived on attention and adulation from others.

Thankfully, they were not interested in airing her story.

Since her passing, several of her Christian friends have told me that she used me in this way because it brought her the recognition, praise, and glory that she so craved. They found it particularly disturbing, since she seemed to have no problem destroying me for her own glorification. It appeared to them to be diametrically opposed to what being a Christian and a mother were all about. Most mothers would defend and protect their child at all costs, but she was more than willing to tie me to the stake publicly and light the fire.

Her reputation as a devout, loving Christian mother was most important to her, and nothing could detract from the "Praise the

Lord" show she put on for others. At the end of her life we had managed to almost mend our relationship, and I have forgiven everything she did to me, but she still would not claim me as her child to anyone she knew. I was always "a friend of the family who was visiting."

I ceased trying to talk about the experiences of my early life, along with the intense pain and suffering I endured. So much of it was at her hands. She never acknowledged any responsibility and the discussion was over before it started.

Closure for my childhood fraught with mental, physical, and verbal abuse on all sides is not something I have ever been able to achieve. Most of it I have just had to let go of as the unresolved mystery of my life.

Other things I still mull over. I try to understand the events, and the people involved, and make some sort of sense out of it. The majority of my life has been spent separated from family, with the exception of my sister who accepted and loved me unconditionally.

All of my life I pretty much felt on the outside of my family looking in. I was never truly a part of it, and that remains to this day. This no longer holds the same sting it once did. I came to accept that while I am related to these people, I will not ever be joined with them as part of a familial unit.

This is due, in large part, to all the misinformation that was fed to my siblings during the many years I was banned from the family. Their perception of me had been formed by my mother, who was not informed in the first place. She sold the family members on her overzealous, ignorant, and fanatical religious ideals. I can't change what they have been taught; I can only live the best example of myself that I know how to be, and the rest in is the hands of my heavenly Father.

I have two brothers left; we do talk sporadically, but there is little in the way of family connection. I clearly sense that I am not a part of them and that they prefer it to be that way. It is not so difficult to withstand the cruelty and rejection of society when you have loving family who supports you. However, it is pure hell without family support.

As I see it, the purpose of family is to shelter, nurture, and love you through your times of torment and hardships as well as times of joy and laughter. When family turns its back on you, it is a battle to exist in world where you are aware that you are unwanted and unloved. Life seems futile, and many good souls are lost because of this.

Because of my personal experience, I desire to be the beacon of love, support, and encouragement for those who feel abandoned, isolated, and marginalized. I believe in the sanctity of all life and I identify as a Christian. I uphold the value of every living being.

There are many things in this life that are complex and difficult to understand. I struggle with issues I don't fully comprehend. In the end, however, I don't believe that it is as important that we understand all the complexities of life as it is to love as Christ taught us to love.

His greatest two commandments were: "to love God with all your heart, with all your soul, and with your entire mind, and with all your being, and then to love your neighbor as yourself."

I try to do that every day.

I often have this vision of Our Lord shaking his head in disgust as his children go about flinging His Word and condemnations at their brothers and sisters who don't measure up to their expectations. They are all the while ignoring His basic commandment of love.

In my experience, I could take anything the world wanted to throw at me, but losing family cut my soul like a hot knife. Trans people are survivors, and we find within ourselves the ability to rise from the ashes of a broken life and emerge anew and stronger from the experience. If transition taught me anything, it was forgiveness and love.

As horrible as my mother was to me, I loved her even when I thought I hated her. I realized one day that I had no power to change her misguided thinking. If I continued to feel anger and resentment the only person I was hurting was myself. No matter how angry I was, I had to be the one who chose to let it all go.

Eventually, I did reach out to her and she responded just before her death. It took many years before change became evident and we could talk without hostility rearing its ugly head. By the end of her life I took care of her and loved her through her illness. Whatever she thought of me no longer mattered; what was really important to me was that I honor God's commandment to love, even someone who had wounded me to the core.

In the end it brought me more blessings that I could have realized and I know now that forgiveness is indeed a priceless gift that is ours for giving and receiving.

Trans folks were not well accepted, and I knew that I didn't identify as Gay. In my early 30's I finally met another woman going through transition, and now had access to hormones. I took some tests at Stanford however they didn't think I was a good candidate for sexual reassignment. I was disappointed. Then, I found another gender study in Ohio. I applied and was accepted. In 1983 I finally received my surgery.

I felt a desire to be of religious service and found the perfect place to serve within the communal life of work and prayer in Nova Scotia Canada. The mother superior was very homophobic, however, and regularly spoke against gays and how they deserved the harm that was inflicted upon them. I was in my late 40's by that time, and my gender was accepted as female by the time I entered the convent.

I very much miss the communal life of prayer, work, and worship that I shared with the sisters, and I would love more than anything to be back among them. I know that God has called me to take what I've learned from them and apply it to those of my brothers and sisters in the trans community who might benefit from it.

It seems a daunting task, and I am not sure where to start, but I am trusting Jesus to lead my path. I hope someday to establish a house of prayer, work, and hospitality in the spirit of St. Benedict for all those who desire to consecrate their lives to His service and are unable to do so within traditional confines of religious life.

I know that to do this, I need to find a member of clergy who is willing to assist in forming a charter Constitution and Rules so that there is proper organization. I want this organization to operate smoothly while respecting the rights and responsibilities of all who wish to unite in this cause. Each one would receive the promises with the vows we make to our calling.

Somewhere I believe there is a need and place for this type of outreach. I just haven't yet figured out the place to begin. There are countless Trans women who selflessly dedicated their lives to Christ's call of service, and the majority of these women live among a society where they don't truly consider themselves an accepted part.

I am still hiding in plain sight, being a care giver to many seniors who have no idea that I used to be "Kim". I am unable to share my story with many, because even after all these years there is a stigma attached to being Transsexual. I am ministering grace to my clients, praying for them and serving them in the name of Jesus. Perhaps one day, my life will make a difference in someone else's life, and we all can be who we really are, loved and accepted by Christ, and showing His love in what we do.

Until then, I hide, and love and serve.

CHAPTER 6

AMUNDAYO DE EDWARDS REGIONAL ADMINISTRATOR FOR TRANS-SAINTS OF THE FELLOWSHIP OF AFFIRMING MINISTRIES

My Introduction: I was introduced to AmunDayo De Edwards at the annual United Church of Christ Justice and LGBT concerns conference at City of Refuge in Oakland, California. His first name is from the Khametic tradition and a part of a longer assigned spiritual name, which is AmunDayo Khepra Oloriiri, meaning son who has a good head, has grand destiny, and self-made joy. Actually I didn't really meet him that night; he was pointed out to me during the service that would install him as the West Coast Regional Minister for the Trans-Saints of the Fellowship of Affirming Ministries. My friend, Bishop Bonnie Radden from Refiners Fire in Long Beach, California had invited me to the service, which turned out to be a divine appointment! AmunDayo De Edwards tuned out to be an Female to Male Trans man with a compelling story he was willing to share

"I take this appointment seriously, understanding the responsibility that comes with such an appointment, for a leader is not good in name only but rather in the work that he or she performs. A great example was set for me by my friend and former West Coast Regional Minister, Miss Bonnie Jean Baker, whose shoes are too big for me to fill. I can only be AmunDayo. Nevertheless, I will take the lessons learned and try to establish footprints of my own, that I and those that I serve and work in collaboration with, will honor the memory of Minister Baker.

There is no doubt the work that needs to be done, for the needs of the Trans community are numerous and our plight is great. At a minimum, and I say this with no exaggeration, we need more resources such as shelters and Homes, counseling facilities, teen-centers and HIV/AIDS resources as well as job skills training and gainful employment just to stay alive." This was not a just well-rehearsed speech but his heart conviction.

He continued: "Numerous Transgendered individuals, espe-cially the younger generations, are often not accepted. They are homeless, hopeless, and live on the streets. Consequently, many re-sort to turning tricks just to have a meal and prostitute themselves for money or a place to stay as they fight to survive.

Although my reality is somewhat different, as I have been blessed to be gainfully employed, to have suitable and secure shel-ter, a loving and supportive wife and son as well as the support of some family members. I believe that the dilemma of one Trans person, is the dilemma of all Trans people.

With such a view, I am passionate about helping to alleviate or eliminate the crisis of the Trans community, bringing vis-ibility to Trans issues and a positive change in attitudes within and without the Trans community. Working in collaboration with other Trans individuals and our allies, my goal is to change policies, and much more as it relates to our position in the community."

I continued with our telephone interview. "Can you tell me about your youth?" I asked. "Did you always know you were a Trans-Man?"

"It is not always easy talking about my youth. I had several unresolved conflicts during that period. The knowledge I have obtained as an adult, has caused me to view my childhood experiences from a new frame of reference.

I understand that my parents did the best they could and I have no desire to assign blame. As a child I was a loner, and I was different in many ways. I was the girl who desired to be my father's son; the girl who wished she had more of a mother-daughter relationship; the church girl rather than the party girl, which also did not make me popular. I was the girl who lived in her brother's shadow; the girl who had certain unexplained feelings for girls rather than boys; and the girl whose parents later divorced. It was difficult. I felt that I belonged nowhere."

He paused, and then continued. "At the age of six I came close to dying after having taken an overdose of a family member's medication that I had often heard tasted like bubble gum. The doctor did not hold out much hope that I would survive, but God said different. I dropped out of high school in my senior year. I had very low self-esteem.

In retrospect, I did not always know that I was a Tran's male. I always felt more masculine than feminine. Back then, a girl like me would be labeled a tomboy. I enjoyed dressing up in my father's clothes when no one was looking. Tasks assigned to men always intrigued me. I would shadow the males in my family every opportunity I got, intently observing how they performed their duties. Afterwards, I would mimic their actions, pretending that I was repairing a car or some type of household item.

I was more convinced that I was male in my early adult years, around the age of 25. This was the age that I had come out as a lesbian and decided to leave the church. Away from the church, I permitted myself to dress and behave as masculine as I felt on the inside. I gave myself a male name and envisioned myself with a male body. Yet, transitioning was far from my mind. I thought I was okay simply dressing and acting as male (stud) rather than being male. I later discovered that my fears of losing those I love, prevented me from seeing the full picture. I thank God for growth and clarity."

His voice lowered. "The journey to me was fraught with a number of unfortunate circumstances, which today I count as some of my most valuable life lessons. I am of the belief that there are no mistakes in life, only opportunities for lessons.

For example, as I tried to live on the "down low" as we say in our community, pretending to be a God-fearing heterosexual woman, I sometimes entertained the attention of male suitors within and without the church. In fact, I was engaged three times.

I was successful in avoiding sexual intimacy in my relationships with men, citing religious piety as my reason for not engaging in such activities. Then, one day I was raped by one of the guys who fancied me."

"I am so sorry that happened to you," I whispered.

"I learned that not living true to oneself can cause an individual to experience traumatic events. This also can result in serious health issues, including neurosis. In fact, there was a period in my life when I suffered from depression, resulting in a short stay in a mental facility. I give glory to God that my bout with mental illness was short lived.

God sent healing to me in many forms, one of which was in the person of Bishop Yvette Flunder. Her life giving words serve as a continuous reminder to live in integrity and accept the freedom given me by God. She told me not to settle for a church that will only use part of me but to find a ministry that will accept all of my gifts. Her words shook my very foundation and caused me to look at my life as a whole. I permanently left the church that I had attended for over 15 years and did some soul searching. During my introspection and time spent listening to God rather than talking, I discovered that not only could I not allow a church to accept only part of me but I too could not permit myself to live as a less than whole individual. This was the beginning of my freedom, spiritually and otherwise, and the preparation for Deiadra (the girl) to make way for AmunDayo (the male) and embrace my life as I am."

"Some people spend a life time and never learn to live authentically." I said. "It's obvious to me that Spirit resides in you."

"I am grateful that this was my journey. I first learned to see and accept myself in spirit before changing the vehicle (body) in which I travelled to earth (was born). I truly believe that successful transitions begin with knowing oneself in spirit; in the same way I believe that transitioning is not continuous.

The process of transition, which is different for each person, depending on influencing factors, will allow the individual to become who he or she is. For me, living as my spirit was created to be is a matter of living my best life rather than a good life."

"I am interested in your spiritual journey, AmunDayo. How did you get involved with City of Refuge? Did you grow up in a Christian Home?"

AmunDayo was quick to respond. "During my break from the Church of God in Christ (COGIC), City of Refuge was one of the open and affirming churches I visited as I searched for answers regarding who I am, and the right or wrong of spirituality and homosexuality. I attended whenever I had an opportunity. I enjoyed the style of worship as it was similar to that which I was accustomed to as a child. The only difference between that which I knew as a younger person and what I was now experiencing, is that, in this new environment, the Word was more affirming and inclusive. I think, in some ways, this is what it means for the Word to be made flesh; it is lived making room for all.

Additionally, the people and the makeup of the families' present were delightfully different in many ways. I could relate to them. I am happy be able to say that my view of what is now The Fellowship of Affirming Ministries was correct. Over time, I have discovered that my view has been enhanced, and I currently view the ministry as both inclusive and expansive.

The first thought that comes to mind as I think about how I got involved with the work of the ministry is that I recently stopped asking myself how I got here and started accepting the fact that I am here. The late Minister Bobbie-jean Baker, whom I loved dearly, asked me to give prayerful consideration to being her assistant for the West Coast Regional Trans Saints Ministry.

My first instinct was to run. I tried to provide every excuse I could find, because I felt inadequate. However, Minister Baker saw through my excuses and told me to keep praying. She trusted that she heard God say that I was to be her assistant. I am happy that she kept her faith in God's voice and that I finally accepted the position.

In part it was my work in the Trans Ministry that aided in my decision to transition. This allowed me to meet some awesome Trans men of God, who took me as their brother and shared their lives with me in spirit and truth and provided models of a healthy transgendered process.

I am a babe in the community, so to speak. I still rely upon the assistance of from both my Trans brothers and Trans sisters to help me in fulfilling this ministry of outreach and to bring about change.

I am blessed to be a part of this community, and I learn something new each day as we engage one with another. The inadequacies I felt that used to consume me with fear were based on what I thought I knew or didn't know. Now I am often reminded of the young David, who with a simple sling and a stone slew the giant Goliath.

My giant is the many challenges and obstacles that face the Transgendered community on the West Coast. Together, we can and we will work for the good of all with the help of the community at large and of the Trans community in the west coast region as well as the Almighty.

As I often stated, I believed I was born under a pew, for my family is very religious. They are fervent worshipers and faithful workers in the church. I am from a lineage of pastors, missionaries, and church musicians from the Baptist, Methodist, and COGIC traditions. I was an aspiring COGIC missionary and a Choir Director. If you understand the theology of these denominations, you could appreciate my struggle, throughout the years, to truly accept that I was other than a heterosexual woman. However, with new knowledge and understanding as well as getting to know God for myself, a lot of things changed, including my theology.

I am rooted in Christianity, yet it may surprise you to learn that I am a Khametic Priest and Interfaith Pastor with the Kindred of ShiEndra under the leadership of Grand Queen MaShiAat Oloya Adedapoidle Tyehimba-Ford.

It is my belief that there is one God but many aspects of the one God that are celebrated in different ways across cultures and time. It seems logical to me this expansion of my theology should include other faith traditions and indigenous spiritual practices. No two people are alike. We may share similarities but we have distinct differences."

"So, tell me how that is fleshed out in your mode of worship." I encouraged him to continue.

"We should not expect that we would all worship alike. I think this is part of a greater plan, so that we would need each other to appreciate the fullness of God and the "All" that God is.

Trans individuals are included in the 'each other.' Like our body, which is made up of many parts with different functions that work in harmony to help us successfully navigate our external world, so too must we come together from various religious and faith traditions to reveal and honor the God we serve. Yet, I display and embrace the charismatic preaching style and hoop-la for which I was conditioned, and love.

Both my choice to transition and my theological beliefs have been the source of many controversial discussions within my family. I have used the word choice on a number of occasions; however, being male is more of a spiritual birth right than a choice to me.

I am supported by some family and friends, but not all. One family friend, a pastor, whom my mother has worked with for years as the church secretary, informed me that the word from God is I will not live long because of my decision to transition.

I am thankful that he does not speak for God. I give thanks for my years lived thus far and for those to come. Still, I am grateful that my family, at least those with whom I am close, has chosen to love me and respect my decision despite their disagreement with my transition.

My very traditional and religious mother has made great strides in her acceptance of me. She took the news about my transition better than I expected. My mother has often credited my growth and happiness as influential factors in her decision to learn something new and to respect individual differences between people regardless of her religious beliefs.

I went from a high school dropout to a college graduate; from living on public assistance to self-sufficiently, from codependency to living independently; from low self-esteem to confidence, from a one-bedroom apartment to a three-bedroom home; and the list goes on. I could shout right here, for there is power in living true to one's self and in living free!"

"I celebrate those achievements along with you, my brother." I smiled to myself.

"There is no mistaking the movement of God in my life. Additionally, my mother seems to be content that I have a relationship with God and carry out my work in the ministry, taking pride in my accomplishments so far. I am grateful that she has on occasion attended church with me and been present for the important events in my life pertaining to ministry.

It is important to note that I want the reality and testimony of all Trans people to be relatively the same as that which I have shared or greater. This is why the church must stand behind its Trans members. It was my faith that sustained me and the support of my church and spiritual communities that kept me going when I faced rejection by society. The church served many roles, including compensating for the lack of family support and love. It is not good enough just to tolerate and include us as members of the church; room must be made to incorporate Trans people in every area of ministry. We have many gifts to bring to the table, and it is my prayer that the church doesn't miss out!"

"I notice that the Trans-saints and affirming ministries is pretty active across the country. Can you share with me some of the projects; goals and outreach plans for your group?"

A broad smile spread across his face as he was happy to bring awareness to the plight of the Trans community in hopes that others may be better informed and moved to render their support.

"My job will be to facilitate the outreach throughout the Western United States." A list of statistics followed: "At least 17% of all hate crimes touch the Trans community, and that is 6 times more than the average experience of reported hate crimes. In San Francisco alone there are over 100,000 LGBT people. Due to the fear in the Trans community, many of the crimes are never reported.

There is reluctance on the part of the media to fully engage with reported violence and how gender identity plays a strong role with some crimes. Trans women are used to being ignored and mocked when reporting violence. Many of these women are homeless; on drugs, or have mental health issues, all without resources for treatment and a safe place to live. There is no safe place even if they have a home, and the gay bars offer little protection from harassment. They are certainly not safe on the streets. Many of those in the Trans community are Asian, Hispanic and African American, which brings in not just issues of the Caucasian society, but cultural influences on gender." He paused. "We are trying to raise awareness and are fighting for our lives as we reach out to the church and ask for help."

He looked at me cautiously. "Are you aware of all the issues we face in the Trans community?"

"No" I admitted.

"There is a lot of transphobia that requires education and exposure to these needs, along with outreach to the community. We are not confused about our mission, no matter how seemingly daunting at times. We are all in this together. Oversimplified, it is clear that we work to alleviate or eliminate the crisis of the Trans community brought about by limited societal thinking and unjust policies. My challenge is to make visible the issues faced by Trans people as we reach out to the community to support us in changing archaic policies and to bridge the gap until such changes are instituted.

The other three individuals who were set aside for ministry outreach at the Trans Saints conference, will work in collaboration with me. We will exchange ideas one with another as we work together to accomplish our goals. We are intentional about exemplifying what it means to treat each other justly, with respect, and love, so that others may join us and follow suit, moving from separation (it is not my issue) to integration (it is our issue)"

His next statement was more of a spiritual challenge to become educated.

"It will take more than the Trans community to effect change. We need the continued support of our allies and support from our churches, communities and various organizations. We invite everyone to the table to learn more about the issues affecting the Trans community and its people, so that they may operate and make decisions from an informed place rather than an uninformed one. Let's close the divide." He waited for his words to sink in. "I can quote statistics about hundreds of deaths each year. That's why there is an International Transgender Day of Remembrance every year and the names are listed as well as how they died. Passing legislation isn't enough, because hatred cannot be wiped out with another law or ordinance in the work place. In the Bay Area we had the first death of a Trans man last year! Just this week a 31-year-old Trans woman was found murdered behind a garbage bin, where she was set on fire! There is no shortage of violence and most of the time, it is passed over or not even reported in the media." Tears ran down his cheeks. "We have to be part of the answer. This has to stop."

"I agree with that!" I choked back the growing lump in my throat. "On a personal note, do you have any experience with oppressive violence? How about your spouse? And I see a child in your FB profile. Is he aware of the dangers you are exposed to on a daily basis?" My questions tumbled out as I thought about the violence against transgendered people across America.

"I've never been physically attacked, yet I am aware that my transition exposes me to the possibility of violence from those who vehemently oppose my decisions. In fact, taking testosterones could place me at risk for several health problems. It is important to understand that the decision to transition is not taken lightly by Trans individuals. We are aware of the numerous risk factors and still we make the decision, for we can no longer live other than whom we believe we are created to be.

My wife and son have been extremely supportive. I love them dearly and hold them close to my heart. My thirteen-year-old son has many questions. My wife and I are very protective of him and do our best to provide him answers. We raise him to be inclusive and accepting of others, 'to think outside the box', live in integrity with self and others, and be open to the path that God has laid before him, whatever that may be. I am proud that my transition affords me the opportunity to live what I teach before my son. I hope that this will positively impact his life and give him the courage to be all that he is created to be. His biggest concern seems to be whether my transition will cause him issues in school. Otherwise, he has adjusted to the pronouns very well and has no trouble calling me Dad and referring to me as he. My son also gives me pats on the back. He still kisses me on the cheeks goodnight and I thoroughly enjoy that. He is aware of the possible dangers I may face and have experienced firsthand the cruelty of individuals when one is different. He is well-spoken, socially adept, spiritually gifted and discerning with a Trans parent and priestess mother. For him, the likelihood that I will be physically hurt is relatively far from his daily thoughts.

At first my wife was unsure if my transition would affect our relationship, but she has never wavered in her support of me. She believes that people should live their best lives, which includes aligning one's body with one's spirit. She is concerned about the risk factors, yet she trusts God. I have heard her say that she also considers herself Trans, for she has made a transition in the way she sees gender, and no longer defines same by what's between a person's legs. As time passes, she is discovering that as I continue to transition my body, she also transitions in her own way. So far, she seems to be enjoying the changes in me.

One of her favorite change is my voice, which has deepened. Priestess Anes-a Anyanwa and I have known each other for almost nine years. I chased her for four of those years, for God told me she was to be my wife. We have been in a serious relationship for the remainder of the years and obtained our domestic partnership in 2012. I have no regrets, for my wife is an amazing woman of God and the love of my life. She is a spiritual healer and prophetess and we work well together in ministry. In fact, recently she has considered the possibility of working to develop better relationship between cisgender and transgender women. A native of the island of Jamaica, she is also burdened with the plight of the LGBTQ people in Jamaica and seeks to make a difference. Trans individuals seem to face more hatred on the island as evidenced by the brutal death of Dwayne Jones, a 16-year-old transgender teenager, who was beaten, shot, stabbed, and ran over by a car.

There is a lot in the news about Uganda and the oppression of the gay/trans community, but in Jamaica, gays and Transgendered men and women are also killed frequently. In many countries, if not universally, Trans individuals risk their lives living out loud and struggle for basic human rights. It's one thing to raise financial support, but so much more is needed in education and advocacy on their behalf. It's the same abroad as it is here. The more visible the Trans community becomes; the more people have to pay attention. It is a larger issue than what bathroom we use, we are fighting for our lives, and every life matters."

"Thank you AmunDayo for sharing your story. I will hold Trans Saints and the Fellowship of Affirming Ministries in prayer, and tell your stories to create awareness in the community. Do you have any last words to share?"

"Just to pray for our outreach, and help us to be visible. Don't be afraid to talk to us and take a stand for justice at every opportunity."

"That is a good reminder for all of us, as we live in this world! Namaste"

VOICES OF GAY MEN

CHAPTER 7

BRYAN BURMA-

Bryan hasn't marched for gay rights, written books, produced songs or any of those types of activities. He is the kind of man you might classify as "ordinary."

"I grew up in the Church of God of Anderson, Indiana. It is a Holiness church, along the lines of the Baptist, or Nazarene. There were a lot of things considered sin, and I tried hard to avoid those things. However, I had one main struggle from my early youth: I was attracted to boys which was absolutely a big "don't" in my churches doctrine. I had many short- term affairs in my youth, and struggled with the guilt. I was told by my family and other church counselors that I would go to hell if I continued on with those relationships. I even debated whether to commit suicide, or get married.

I decided to get married to prove to myself and others that I was "straight". My wife and I had a daughter together. However, inside my heart, I knew that I was attracted to men. I came out to my wife in 1991. She thought she could "cure" me from my homosexual attractions, however it ended up that I only put her through hell for all the years of our marriage.

She encouraged me to date men because she thought I was bisexual. It turned out when my wife said I needed to go get a boyfriend, and I did, that she couldn't handle the jealously. She had also recommended counseling which I did, but after 13 years, I decided to get a divorce. We finalized our divorce in 1996."

Bryan continued, "I have spent my entire life trying to be comfortable with who and what I am. I accepted Jesus into my life when I was 5 years old, and felt a call to serve God. I struggled with inferiority feelings and didn't think I was acceptable for ministry because I was Gay. All I ever heard at Church was that someone couldn't be Christian and Gay.

He reflected, "I left the church for many years. Many longtime friends walked away from me, rather than address my homosexuality or my divorce. My Pastor once walked on the other side of the street rather than engage me in conversation when we were in the same area. It really hurt my feelings and caused me deep emotional pain and great harm.

However, my isolation from the church did not extend to my personal relationship with God. I still believe in prayer and spiritual gifts of discernment and healing. I know that God still hears me, and answers prayers on my behalf. He didn't dump me off the edge of the world. I kept asking Him, "What the hell is going on? People tell me I'm condemned, but You still answer my prayers!"

When I was younger I remember having a toy rubber doll, that I could stretch the arms and legs and the body in different directions. Years later as I reflected on my childhood, and remembered that doll, I had an epiphany. When I 'came out'...I snapped into place! Everything was the way it was intended to be, and I was finally whole. I continued to pursue a spiritual path and seek God's will as to where I could be used by Him.

One of my spiritual gifts is a strong intuitive discernment, and I can often see what's going on with someone in the Spirit. I've been able to minister to many people with this gift. The Bible states that the gifts and calling of God are irrevocable, and that once given, they remain active. I still believe that to be true.

The more that I studied the Scriptures and researched the meaning of words about homosexuality; I knew I was on the right track in understanding my sexuality. I am now 53 years old, and more convinced than ever, that God created me just as I am, and He doesn't make mistakes!

I come from many generations of ministers in the Church of God- Anderson Indiana. My Great, Great Grandma was one of the first circuit preachers, contemporary with John Wesley. All of my religious teaching has its roots in the Holiness movement. I have now come to be at peace with my sexual orientation and my relationship with God.

I was with one partner for eight and a half years, and together, we worked to support Christian ministry outreaches by promoting them with web site hosting. It was a calling I very much enjoyed. I am very knowledgeable with computers and for several years we did this as a ministry of helps. However, sites like Facebook have made a lot of private websites unnecessary. I no longer feel called to work in that field.

This work could be done from almost anywhere, and I lived in a small town in Michigan. The weather had a negative impact on my breathing and I decided to I move from Michigan to Colorado. This happened a little over three years ago. The relationship with Harry, my partner for almost eight years, was terminated shortly after we arrived in Colorado.

I was hoping the change of location would improve my health. I have severe asthma, and a heart condition that has plagued me all my life. The arrhythmia in my heart got 10 times worse on medication that was prescribed to help my condition. My heart had only half as much blood as it should have, and I almost died. The doctors prescribed an inhaler, which is causing me to go blind. I have also suffered epileptic grand mal seizures from my youth.

The doctors tell me I am a walking miracle having experienced over 175 seizures in a short period of time.

Even in the midst of my health problems I felt the call of God on my life to further my ministry by being ordained. The Open Door Community Church in Denver acknowledged my spiritual calling, and I am now an ordained pastor.

I have a relationship with a new partner and we have been together almost four years. He identifies as spiritual, not Christian. His life has many phases of faith, and he is still finding himself. We give each other a wide birth to be who we are, and I don't define for him how to experience God. I am learning that God is so much more than I can define, and I am content to keep growing in faith and in our relationship

I have one sister who is still in the process of accepting me as a gay man. She is an RN and is in the Who's Who in nursing. She has difficultly reconciling her understanding of the Scriptures on homosexuality with what she views as "my choice." I am content not to debate the issue.

I also have a brother who is an Apostolic Pentecostal, and I don't debate with him either. He acknowledges that I am a Christian, and is content to let the Holy Spirit convict me if need be.

My mother passed away two years ago from Alzheimer's disease, so it is not an issue with whether she knew and accepted me.

I have been out to my dad for 16 years, and we don't really discuss my sexual orientation.

I have been in a time of transition with my church relationship. I have been attending the United Methodist church here in Denver, which was a welcoming congregation. They just closed the church due to a drop in membership. I feel a new direction is needed for my life, and wherever that ends up, I need to feel I have a place of service.

As a gay man who also embraces my faith, I am committed to doing all I can to promote the message that God loves everyone, and we are all His children. Many gay people I meet are no longer interested in following a God they have been told doesn't love and accept them.

My ministry is to change that perception.

CHAPTER 8

ED MEYERS, 50
HIV POSITIVE

I met Ed in 1985, when he found a book I had written on the internet. I began counseling relationship with him, which developed into a friendship which has remained strong through the years.

He told me, "I had just broken up with a lover of many years, and was not ready to hear this crushing news. My life changed forever, and although I continue to live with HIV, it is much different than when I was young. Here is my story.

It was in December, 1993 that my six month tests came back positive.

I had been volunteering at a group in Pittsburg, PA called the Pittman Study for gay and bisexual men. It has been a way to meet other gay men, and be in a support group. Part of the requirements for taking part was to be tested for HIV every six months.

I had engaged in anonymous sex, and had lots of sexual encounters. One person told me that he was positive, yet we had unprotected sex. I was a dummy for not using protection. I liked being with different people, and I wasn't smart about how we had sex.

When I found out I was positive, I wasn't angry. I was just barely thirty years old, and I was afraid of dying. I had no one to blame but myself. I didn't blame God; it was all on me and my behavior. I was smart enough to know that there are consequences to my behavior.

I remember thinking that I needed to find someone to talk with who would not condemn me, and would walk me through the depression I was experiencing. I talked with many pastors and found them less than helpful. Rev. Darlene always listened to me and did not pass judgment on what I had done, or what I would do in the future. We had many long phone conversations and she always prayed with me and told me that God loved me.

I became more hopeful for longevity as I was put on a cocktail regiment of drugs to treat the symptoms. The treatment for AIDS has improved through the years, and while there is not yet a cure, people are living many years longer than anyone expected.

I am currently on a cocktail of drugs, including Norvir; Reyataz; and have been on Truvada for the past two years. I have good CD 4 count (T-cells). Currently, mine are *500 to 700. My viral load is undetectable and that is very good.* The side effects are minimal, mostly diarrhea, and I can plan my life around those reactions.

I am bi-polar, and take bi polar meds also, mostly Lithium. They had me taking Abilify, but it made me feel like a zombie, so I quit taking it.

I do have a Psychiatrist, a woman, but I'm not impressed with her. She listens to me, but isn't very helpful with positive suggestions. I go to see her when the pressure builds up inside me or when I get into trouble and act out sexually, or when I explode in anger. I expect her to be more interactive, and perhaps one day I will seek out a new therapist.

I have always been fearful of adults because of the experiences I had in the children's Home, where my parents sent me when I was 9 years old. I am basically afraid of people and won't talk until I'm sure I can trust them. I suppose this stems from the fact that I was raised in children's homes from age 9 to age 17. My mother couldn't handle me because I was "high strung and uncontrollable with angry outbursts" and felt I needed to be in a controlled environment. I was not diagnosed as bi-polar until years later.

I lived in Hamilton Ohio while I was in junior high. I don't remember how I ended up there, but it must have been through the influence of the Children's Home. After high school, I attended Villanova N.E Christian Junior College. It was connected with Church of Christ. I wanted to be a Bible teacher because I really loved the Bible. My comprehension skills and lack of discipline, combined with a lack of confidence in my surroundings, caused me to drop out after a year.

I was strongly attracted to boys and enjoyed sexual exploration from the time I was five years old. A neighbor kid and I messed around, and it always felt comfortable. Even in college, I was a very active sexual being. Often, I would find sexual partners in the bath houses and go to other pickup places from time to time. I didn't feel a lot of guilt. I knew it wasn't right and could be dangerous, but I couldn't help it, and it became a compulsive addiction.

I talked to plenty of Christian people from time to time, who condemned the sin, but not me. I always felt their acceptance was conditional and didn't really trust them

I'm not with anyone at this point in my life, and I have cut down on my sexual activity due to my HIV status. Sometimes I slip and act out, but not very often. My last lover was Larry who I met in 1986. We were together for 4 years and decided we made better friends than lovers. We are still friends today.

My mom is still alive and battling cancer. She either doesn't know or want to ask why things are difficult for me. I love her, but we can't talk about anything important. I suppose in many ways; I feel her love is also conditional. My Dad was born in 1917 and died in '82. He and I never talked about me being gay. He was pretty much emotionally absent in my life. I have resigned myself to knowing that is the way it was, and nothing can ever change my past loneliness. When I hear about loving families who accept their gay children, it creates a special sadness.

In our area of Pennsylvania, there is a lot of violence against gays, which makes me afraid to go out alone into the community. The cops are pretty supportive, and don't harass anyone just because they are gay.

I have been a volunteer at the Shepherd Wellness program in Pittsburg for several years. It was established in 1987, and it is a supportive setting for those infected and affected by AIDS. They have a compassionate outreach to help people die with dignity. They also have frequent Dinners and have established a safe time and place for fellowship. At first they just rented space, now, the outreach has purchased their building. I often just go down and talk to other men who also have AIDS. I find it helpful for myself and them.

I was raised in the Church of Christ--- not a Pentecostal church. I don't have a very good relationship with God. I know the Bible says God loves me no matter what, however I just don't feel that He accepts me, because I am Gay. I no longer go to Church for much the same reason. I feel that if I told the people at church that I was queer and had AIDS, they would reject me. I read my Bible at Home and listen to tapes, but that's about it for my spiritual journey.

Learning to trust God has been hard. I hope someday I can come to the place where I really know that He loves and unconditionally accepts me. I'm not afraid of dying any longer, but I want to live as long as I can.

I know in my head that I'm a child of the King of Kings, but in my heart I feel like I am fighting the Devil, and sometimes, it's me!

CHAPTER 9

JOE AND SEAN:
THE MUSIC PLAYED ON.

"My name is Joe Hogue. I was born on May 9th 1965 and I was raised in Plant City, Florida.

My father was a music minister and I followed in his footsteps. I spent much of my childhood accompanying my family on the piano. It seemed I had many natural talents and I was a quick study in picking up music. All of my family was involved with music or singing at the church. I was the middle child of three and as each of my siblings came along, we all developed our talents in the area of music. Our family band was much in demand, and most of my youth was spent playing music in church.

After high school, I received a full ride scholarship to South Florida University. I looked forward to the challenges of college; however, the challenges at home were more pressing. I had to return home after just two weeks into the semester, due to our family vehicle breaking down. I had the only other vehicle, which my parents now needed. My college experience was finished, and I never returned to that path. It seemed that my first love of music was in fact where I was being called.

At 18, I started touring with Christian singing group, TRUTH. Along with this group I performed in over 350 concerts within one year. My musical talents were quickly acknowledged and I moved to Nashville Tennessee to tour with a Christian solo artist. The next two years were like a dream come true.

By my early 20s I was being hired to play piano and sing for recording sessions throughout Nashville. My musical talents quickly evolved into writing, arranging and producing for many artists. Time in the studio allowed me to get my name known in the industry, however it didn't fulfill my desire to perform on my own.

I soon started a boy band with my brother and his best friend Todd Collins. Our group was called 3D, and was successful right from the beginning. We were offered a record deal with RCA records, but I did not sign the contract because I felt that it restricted my growth potential with all the limitations contained in the contract.

I left the band and throughout 90s I produced nearly every Christian artist that existed at the time. My credits garnished Grammy awards and many Dove Awards for my clients. My music and artists were selling multiple gold and platinum records exceeding 25 million in sales. I was on the fast track to success, working with such notable artists as DC talk, Michael W Smith, Ray Boltz, Carman, Michael McDonald, BeBe and CeCe Winans. I was not satisfied with just producing records and soon expanded into composing. I was a Nashville success story and it seemed that I had everything that life could offer. I also became an Emmy award winning composer garnering A&E their very first Emmy for composing the biography theme. It seemed that my life was totally blessed by God, and all I needed to complete the picture, was a wife. This seemed to be the great American dream. I never disclosed the deep inner conflicts that plagued my thoughts when the music stopped.

In 1989, I married my high school sweetheart, and we had our only son in 1992. At first, at least on the surface, everything seemed ideal however the underlying struggle with sexual attractions and thoughts toward men, did not help my relationship with my wife. I was well established in the music world and finances were not an issue. The only issue was trying to embrace my true sexual identity, and I couldn't talk about it."

Sean's Story

Sean Petersen, also grew up in a pastor's family. He recalls, "I was born in Minneapolis, Minnesota in1977. I also was the middle child of three. Just like Joe, I gravitated towards music at a young age. I grew up singing and playing drums in the church. Ironically many of the songs that I loved and performed were songs that Joe Hogue had produced.

As a teenager, I was not allowed to listen to secular music so I owned about 15 records that Joe had produced. We didn't know one another; however, Joe was a big part of my dream to become a Christian artist, a writer and producer. In my late teens, I moved to Nashville to attend Belmont University, not knowing that Joe also lived there. Later, I turned down a scholarship to study classical music at the University of Northern Iowa.

I wanted to pursue my love of a more commercial sound.

I was born into a generation where heterosexual marriage was the plan for everyone, and just like Joe, I also married a girl. She was Southern Belle from Kentucky and we were introduced by my father with the intent of Christian marriage. I embraced my father's desires, and soon, I was married to the girl of my father's dreams.

However, Joe and I not only shared a similar background, but a similar struggle about our sexuality. Our strong Southern Baptist and Wesleyan church teachings left no flexibility to explore other options for love. We were on a parallel course of understanding our sexuality, yet we weren't aware of each other.

As we talked later, we both believed that we would need to keep our struggles with our sexuality a secret for a lifetime. Because of our faith, living an "out" gay life was not even an option. To complicate things, there was the small detail of finding ourselves in marriages to women. Our hidden secrets were not fixed by those marriages, and the pressure of our secret longings led us to the internet in search of answers.

In the year 2000, we found ourselves involved in online meetings with each other. It was the first time either of us had openly talked about our desire to be with a man. Sharing these secrets lead to other secrets all carefully withheld from our wives and our church contacts. Our intent was not to hurt anyone, but we knew it was inevitable.

After about a month of telephone and email contacts, Joe return from Toledo where he had been producing a live record called New Season. We finally arranged a face to face meeting...

There was an instant bond, and we quickly became very close and began working together on music recording projects. The intensity of our friendship was electrified, like having your cake and eating it too.

Our families knew each other so our relationship was kept on the down low. We were able to see each other but the intensity was such that we were sure our feelings would soon be obvious. We fell in love!" Sean recalls the frustrating feeling of loving someone and knowing that you will never be able to be together. Our kind of love was just not part of God's plan as we understood it. "It just seemed like an impossible situation. Our Christian faith was only part of the problem."

Sean also recalls "We knew our Christian families would have a very hard time with our relationship and not be accepting of a homosexual relationship. We lived in the South, and attitudes were pretty strong about 'what the Bible said or didn't say' on those matters"

Then, there was our wives and Joe's son. We hadn't expected to fall in love with one another, however even after just days; we had this connection that was far deeper than what we had experienced with our wives. It was the feeling of having known each other for our entire lifetimes.

Our feelings continued to deepen and we were not only increasingly falling deeper in love with each other, but also dealing with a deeper internal conflict. It was increasingly obvious to both of us that our wives deserved to experience true love as well and that kind of love was a love neither of us was able to give to our wives. It was time to admit that fact and do the right thing. Those conversations with our spouses were painful, and devastating, however we couldn't live with our secret any longer.

It was truly the best of times and the worst of times. After much discussion and prayer, we both proceeded with divorce actions. We needed to explore what our relationship could become as Christian men who loved one another.

The next several years were riddled with court dates, lawsuits, contempt orders, attorneys, police calls, custody battles, restraining orders and even jail time.

Joe's wife placed a restraining order against Joe, in which he was prohibited from exposing his son to "his gay lifestyle" and his gay lover/lovers. Therefore, every visitation that Joe had with his son I had to move out of the house during that time. It was the only way to allow the visit. That was a very painful time in both of our lives. At the same time Judge Robert E Lee Davies ordered Joe to pay $5100 every month in support payments, which soon bankrupted him.

Joe soon began to lose all of his Christian music jobs as the word spread about his personal life, and our relationship.

Compounding the situation, Joe's son, who was now eight years old, began to ask questions about why he had divorced his mom. This resulted in Joe telling him the truth about being a gay man.

His initial response was very understanding, at least as understanding as an eight-year-old could be about this emotionally charged situation. However, after returning from visiting his mother's family, Joe's son's attitude abruptly changed. He began misquoting Bible verses and completely spouting incorrect and insane statistics about the sin of homosexuality.

His comments were nothing like a child would say. Joe soon found himself in a criminal contempt case with his eight-year-old son on the stand testifying against him.

He and his son had always had a great relationship and this broke Joe's heart. At one time their relationship had been the envy of all the neighborhood children. The court didn't view their past relationship as a positive factor and as a result, Judge Robert E Lee Davies sentenced Joe to 2 days in jail for his honesty about our relationship.

The judge stretched beyond the law, and he also stripped Joe of all parental decision-making rights because he was a gay man. He also took away time each week from visitation. The judge further ordered that the child not be told about the sentencing. Joe was deeply grieved as he posted bail.

The judge's ruling also allowed Joe's wife to move the child 12 hours away to live in Florida. Joe appealed the judgment which ultimately was overturned; however, he had to involve the ACLU in order to get a fair judgment. The damage had already been done as far as his loving and caring relationship with his son was concerned. It is still painful to this day.

Joe was left in Nashville with no work and now, no family. It was apparent that we needed to move, which we did in 2004. We moved to Los Angeles where we began to work with various secular artists as well as the LGBT music community. We were starting at the bottom, trying to regain our credibility as producers and musicians.

Joe had lost nearly every contact from his 20-year career in Nashville. We had to rebuild not only our own relationship, but our professional music base.

It was a new start as a team, and it was a new season in our lives. We continued to produce music together, becoming known as HiTPLAY in 2006. We had to reinvent ourselves through the music industry's ever-changing reality. We managed to gain several Billboard hits and continued pursuing artistry of our own.

We were restoring our personal dreams of becoming recording artists and this was the new season to make it happen. We were coming together as a team, musically and personally.

It was also a new season in our relationship. Unexpectedly we found ourselves experiencing an impromptu wedding ceremony. The wedding took place at 4 pm on Halloween in 2008, behind our house, by the pool with just a few friends and our beloved Saint Bernard, Roland in attendance. This was also right before the prop 8 elections in California. When we saw that the polls numbers didn't look good for marriage equality and we decided it was now or never.

When the election ended, our fears were correct and marriage equality was once again denied to Californians as a result. We, however, were now among 18,000 legally married gay couples in the state.

Our personal journeys are finding fulfillment as we are part of a vibrant church in Long Beach, California, doing what we love… playing music. We are loved by our community at Glory Tabernacle which recently changed its name to Glory Center..

Joe's relationship with his son would often go up to a year at a time with agonizing silence. Our prayer had been that with time it would be mended and restored to a loving relationship. While their relationship continues to improve there are painful memories that linger. Joe's son is no longer a child. He was married in 2013 and as he has matured into adulthood, his understanding has increased regarding same-sex unions and what it means to be gay in America. It is sometimes difficult to leave the rigidity of beliefs of the Bible belt teachings and experience the freedom of God's unconditional love.

The one relationship that has been healed is with Joe's father, Joseph Randolph Hogue Sr.

We were able to see him just prior to his death in 2008. Joe was in tears when his dad apologized for the things that were said against us through the years. Joe received the resolution and healing from his dad that he needed to move on with his life.

His dad died during his first night at a professional care facility

We are anticipating our first HiTPLAY record release in 2016. It's a new season and it's a new day, and we are part of the new sounds that reach our world. Our faith is alive and well, and the music plays on!

LONG TERM COMMITTED
RELATIONSHIPS

CHAPTER 10

BOB AND LLOYD- DISPELLING THE MYTHS

I 'm sure you've read the false statistics or heard them proclaimed in pulpits across the country: Gay relationships don't last! Perhaps a couple of years, but even if men are still together after three years, they usually bring in other relationships for sexual pleasure. They are never monogamous, and can have as many as 300 contacts in their lifetime! They cannot procreate, and are often pedophiles and can't be trusted around children. If any of this sounds familiar; please meet Bob and Lloyd.

This couple would be the first to say that they are not perfect. They are, however, in a committed relationship that has so far lasted 47 plus years! They fell in love on the night they met, and it has only gotten better since then.

Both Bob and Lloyd had married women in their early twenties, and each had a child. They both lived with a lot of regret over having gotten married just because it was expected that all young men would get married, have children, and grow old with their spouse. Their wives did love them, however, that love was not reciprocal. Back in the day, there was no other pathway for marital happiness. Even in Vancouver Canada, marriage was the dream of all young people. There was one major problem: Neither Bob or Lloyd enjoyed the sexual relationship with their wives.

As for pedophilia, of course, neither of them desired sexual contact with children. They simply longed to find their life's fulfillment with another man.

Lloyd recalls: "As I look back on our journey the first 20 years was spent mostly looking at life from the bottom of a bottle." The alcohol didn't dull the pain or the feeling that no one could love them because they were gay.

"In 1986, things got so bad for me that I went on a drinking binge. All I could think of was that even God didn't love me. I had been listening to Jimmy Swaggert on television, and while I loved his music, on every program Swaggert would walk up and down the platform attacking homosexuals, saying they would all burn in hell! I kept drinking, screaming in my mind that 'I *can't take it any longer*'. I got into my Buick Riviera and began to drive across Vancouver on the freeways, until at 75 miles an hour, I hit a concrete barrier.

The firemen had to remove me from the wreck with the 'Jaws of life'. They thought I was surely dead inside the tangled metal. I was in a coma for three days. When I woke up in the hospital, one of the many thoughts I had: '*I can't even kill myself right!*' Then, I saw my darling Bob leaning over me. I was thrilled to be alive. I became more committed to spiritual guidance after that accident. '*Your hand is upon my life for a reason, Lord, or I wouldn't still be here. What do you have for us to do?*'

Over the following months, Bob and I spoke often about what we should be doing with our lives. I was more committed to spiritual goals at this point. It was on New Year's Eve, 1988 when we both quit drinking. We began to make plans without our former support group of drinking buddies. My life was about to change in ways I couldn't imagine.

I scanned several travel magazines as we began to plan a vacation. The name Phoenix kept popping up and I felt drawn to that area. Bob thought I was crazy because Phoenix was in the desert. I just knew we needed to go to that area, and insisted that was our next vacation. We booked a wonderful hotel in Scottsdale, Arizona, just outside of Phoenix. It was pleasant enough, but there was still a void in my heart. *Had I not really heard from God?*

We were sitting by the hotel pool one Saturday, and Bob read me an article in the local paper about something called a Holy Union taking place the next day at the Metropolitan Community Church. It was 1988, and we were not aware of these gay unions taking place in church. I suggested we find the church and attend the ceremony.

Bob's response was immediate. "Now I know you're crazy. We haven't been inside a church in over 20 years."

I heard an inner voice saying, '*You need to go. This is important.*'
I asked directions to the street where the church was located, and early Sunday morning we headed off to find it.

We got lost and had no idea where we were. I had the feeling that God was driving and was in control of our journey. I took a few turns and was on a narrow street with scary people standing on the sidewalk. Suddenly, we were in front of a small church with the name, "Casa de Cristo Evangelical Church."

We were quite nervous about going inside, but the beautiful music seemed to draw us in closer. They were just finishing up the 'first' service, so we decided to go up the street for coffee, and return for their second service.

When we arrived back an hour later we were met by the sweetest lady with a huge angel smile and open arms. She introduced herself as Betty and encouraged us to enter God's house and be changed forever more.

Two broken gay men walked through those doors, but by the end of the service we were indeed changed. The church was filled with gay and lesbian people, who sang with the voices of angels, and seemed to glow with peace and a special anointing in worship. My soul was transformed with wonder.

After the service, Bob and I moved to the fellowship hall and met some of the people. The pastor approached us with a smile and a handshake. He introduced himself as Fred Pattison and explained he had been a Baptist Minister. He had left that church several years earlier because he hadn't been accepted due to his sexual orientation Fred invited us back for the evening service which, he said, was more casual. There would be a time of sharing

We agreed to think about it, but had no real intention of returning. We drove back to the hotel and talked about our experience. Both of us agreed we had been deeply moved by the morning service and that we felt a bond with Rev. Pattison.

We decided to return that night and during the worship service, while everyone was singing the song, <u>We are standing on Holy</u>

Ground, both Bob and I gave our lives to the Lord. Neither of us had any idea where that would lead.

Upon our return to Vancouver, both of us became increasingly dissatisfied with our jobs. We sought out the local Metropolitan Community Church as a place of worship and direction. One night while I was at work, a young woman approached me. She asked why Bob and I were still working.

"What are you talking about?" I responded. "I've been working at this same government job for over 20 years and have my pension to consider."

Her response was immediate. "I have this strong feeling that you should be in ministry. Please pray about it."

Those words seemed to come out of the blue. *Ministry? How would that work?* I pondered her words and talked with Bob about her unsolicited message.

A short time later, I was sitting in the living room when Bob came down stairs. He had a strange look on his face. "Today is the day, isn't it?"

I didn't need to ask what he was referring to. I quietly responded. "Yes, it is." It was August 1990, and that day we left our secure jobs to follow where God would lead us. We committed to a six-month time period to search for our place in ministry.

We decided to return to Phoenix, where our calling had first drawn us to be of service. Bob has been blessed with a beautiful singing voice, so we decided to step out in the field of music.

We contacted nursing homes and the Metropolitan Community Church where we could minister in music and testimony.

During the next six months, we studied under several dynamic Bible pastors who held classes at the church. We immersed ourselves in bible teaching attending services every time the doors opened. We discovered that not all Metropolitan Community churches understand and experience the teachings of Jesus Christ in the same way.

When we returned to Vancouver after six months, we were disappointed with the teachings of the MCC where we had been attending prior to Phoenix. Our understanding has increased and our hunger to know God's word was stronger than before. In April 1991 we felt led to begin worshiping at Liberty Church. Pastor Johnson and his wife Shirley had been called as pastors, and they had a strong belief in living as Jesus would in the world today.

Bob continued to be used in the area of music, while my heart was touched with those in the "ex-gay" movement. I was confident in my sexual orientation and believed that God had created me as a gay man. I didn't understand those who were engaged in a struggle to accept or reject their homosexuality. This conflict of being gay and Christian was just emerging as a major issue in churches across America. Canada was no exception to the discussion.

One day I came across a little booklet at a church booth. It was the "testimony" of a man named Frank Shears. It described in depth how he had overcome his homosexuality and was leading an ex-gay ministry in Vancouver. As I read his story, I felt a deep burden to pray for Frank. He was obviously conflicted and confused, no matter what his book proclaimed. I added him to my daily prayer list.

A few months later, I noticed a man sitting in the back pew at church. He was weeping throughout the service. I prayed silently for him. On the next Bible study the following Tuesday, he was at the service. I was impressed with his knowledge of Scripture, and how he participated in the discussion.

I started up a conversation by asking where he attended church before coming to Liberty.

"Burnaby Christian Fellowship", he responded.

I knew that church because of their ex-gay ministry. "What do you think of this guy, Frank Shears?"

He quietly responded. "I am Frank Shears."

In the weeks and months that followed, we had many conversations, and became close friends. Frank had been diagnosed with AIDS, and was dealing with his impending death. A month before he died, CBC did an interview with him for national television. In that interview, he said the only regret he had was telling so many young gay people that they could and should change. He knew in his heart that there was no possibility of them ever changing.

It was through my relationship with Frank that I became aware of the intense struggle to reconcile one's sexuality and spirituality. My heart has been touched to reach out to all who are conflicted, with the message that God loves you just as He created you, and if that is as a homosexual person, you can celebrate your sexuality and your spirituality.

I was honored to speak before the House of Commons Sub Committee in 2003. They were considering the issue of same sex marriage not just domestic partnership status

This is my testimony: "'God made me who I am. He knew who I was even before I was born, and I believe he set the path and my destination as to who my partner was going to be throughout my life. I am who I am. I am what God made me." In my testimony, I also shared that "I happen to think that my being a homosexual is the way God made me. I believe when I was wrong was when I married a woman. I believe it was then that I was "out of the norm."

"I did something that was abnormal for who I was. God made me a homosexual. That's what I believe. I believe I contradicted God's law when I married my wife."

"Don't get me wrong, I'm glad I have children. I'm glad I have grandchildren. It's a privilege in that respect. I happen to believe that being a homosexual is the way God made me. Because of that, I believe the time when I was wrong is when I married a woman.'"

I paused and looked at the court. "I did something that was abnormal for who I was. That's what I believe. I believe I contradicted God's law in that respect."

"Since we gave our lives to the Lord in 1988, we have met so many broken people in our community. They weren't broken because of their sexuality but because they were Christian and a pastor or church elder had falsely told them that they were an abomination in the eyes of God. They were then recruited into a form of change ministry, otherwise known as ex-gays.

I must tell you that I have yet to meet anyone who was once gay but is now heterosexual. However, I have met many who have pretended to be healed or changed, only to find out a short time later that they still had homosexual feelings and attractions. These ex-gay ministries have taken a toll on gay and lesbian youth. Many have committed suicide, and many others have either poured acid on their genitalia or caused severe damage with a knife or razor. Yet these ex-gay groups still flourish in society. It is time we legalized homosexuality and gave everyone the right to live their truth."

The courtroom was very quiet. "I usually have an opinion on almost everything, and this is one of them. There's a standing comment that I have often heard from pastors. It's getting a little boring now. I hear God created Adam and Eve, not Adam and Steve. Well, I have news for them. God also created Adam and Steve."

"Both Bob and I have been married to women. But the marriage couldn't be carried on because we realized that we had a different sexuality. I'd like to make it clear that I'm not talking about sex. I'm talking about sexuality. That's our inner being--our sexuality. If we had no sex from today onward, we're still going to be homosexuals. Nothing will change that.'"

Although that testimony was given many years ago, Lloyd and Bob have been in a true marriage, a union of hearts for over forty-five years. Lloyd is now in his early seventies and Bob is in his mid-sixties, and they are more in love than when they met so long ago.

They have proven that same-sex marriage can not only last, but it can flourish. It should also be mentioned that Bob and Lloyd, along with seven other couples in British Columbia, eight couples in Ontario, and one in Quebec, were responsible for winning the right of same-sex couples to marry in Canada.

The battle started in the courts in 2000, and in four short years same-sex marriage was legal across Canada. It was predicted by some that God would destroy Canada if same-sex marriage were accepted. However, the sky hasn't fallen. Instead, same-sex marriage is hardly mentioned any longer. We just call it marriage.

CHAPTER 11

VENERABLE JANGCHUP PHELGYE
MEANING: ABOUNDING COMPASSION
A GAY BUDDHIST MONK

JangChup Phelgye and I met recently when we were both panel speakers at John F. Kennedy University in San Jose, California. The group was a graduating class of therapists who wanted to interact with experienced gay and lesbian persons who work with the Lesbian, Gay, Transgendered, and Bisexual community. Their focus was how we as people of faith interact and counsel those in the Queer Community.

We were asked to reflect upon our own spiritual journey with Queerness and how comfortable we had become in our integration of our sexual identity with our faith life. Also, how we communicate that with those we counsel.

When I met JangChup, I admitted my ignorance not only of his beliefs, but of what to call him. I wasn't sure how to interact with this man in a robe, and silently prayed that my Pentecostal, Evangelical Pastor image (I was wearing my clerical collar) would not offend him. I decided to listen and learn from his life.

I discovered that we were the same age, and that we had shared a lot of gay history events in common.

JangChup began to share about his life.

"We live in this world, but we really don't know who anyone is in their soul. We all want to be accepted for whom we are, but so often, we don't even know who we are. Life is very complicated. There will always be something external to focus on, besides our souls. For me, it was academic studies.

I earned my BA at the University of California at Berkeley, and my first Masters at Teachers college Columbia University. I was also a counselor at Queens College in New York, as well as Yale in Connecticut. I did post doctorate work at Oxford in England. I was on a search to know myself, and I hoped to find my answer through education.

I am 71 years old, and my 'knowing' didn't come together for me until I embraced Buddhism twenty years ago. I was in my early fifties at the time. After that initial contact, three years later, I began my practice in a Tibetan Buddhist monastery where I ordained. That religious order moved from Tibet to its current location and established a monastery in Southern India. It has been over twenty years since I took my vows.

My path up until that time was filled with a lot of experiences of rebellion and activism for civil rights. For example, in 1964 Berkeley went through a student rebellion that is still talked about today. I was in my twenties at the time and desperately trying to find my place in the world.

Several students from the University who had been active in the civil rights movement went to Mississippi to join what they thought were nonviolent protests for the summer. They were committed to being part of the solution in standing against oppression. When they returned to Berkeley, they discovered that the injustice in the South was also alive and well in Berkeley and throughout the Bay area. The Free Speech Movement was born from that environment. I tried to navigate the political unrest and also remain focused on earning my degree. Education was the area where I sought to quiet my inner conflicts, and it became increasingly difficult to do so.

Human rights were at the forefront of the protests, and I was dealing with my own emerging battle of understanding myself as a gay man. It seemed easier for me at that time to focus on others' civil rights, rather than my own. It was after all, the 1960's.

I graduated from Berkeley and enrolled at Columbia University to pursue a Teaching Masters in Development Psychology. Again, I was looking to be part of the solution to the conflicts of the human condition.

It was a privilege to have Margaret Mead as my advisor during those years. She was aging, and the University came to her with the suggestion that she might consider retirement. Her response, "I may die, but I am not going to retire!" She passed away in 1978, and it was a great sadness to me, as she had deeply influenced my thinking about life.

In the late 1960's I earned my first Masters in educational psychology, and then went on to counsel at Queens College in New York. I earned another Master's Degree at Yale, in environmental design. And yet my life purpose wasn't taking shape as I anticipated. I loved Psychology; however, there were so many unanswered questions on my own journey, and I continued my search for answers.

While a student at Oxford, I experienced a huge emotional crash. Education and academics no longer made me feel whole. I quietly changed directions, and began writing fiction. Shortly afterwards, I returned to the United States and settled in New York during the 1960's, where I found a comfort in the urban gay environment.

In 1969 I was on the outskirts of the gay culture. While I was not present on the very day, I was aware of the bar in the village called the Stonewall Inn.

The police harassed and raided this and other meeting places for the gay community. The gay and transgendered patrons were usually arrested, sometimes identified and attacked, but always booked and released.

On this day in June, and for a lot of different reasons, just one of which was they had been bullied long enough, the drag queens and Trans community led the resistance, and fought back. Many of these were street kids, and they knew how to speak up. Whether or not it was a contributing factor, and some reports say it was, this was the weekend that Judy Garland had died, and the drag community felt her loss.

There were many smaller groups that joined the opposition, as the word spread of the growing resistance.

I belonged to a men's group of academics, and we joined with the larger community. It didn't make a difference if you were from the streets or the university setting, we were all involved in the protests. The Stonewall riots made national news, and they are still looked on as the beginning of Gay Pride events that mobilized the LGBT community and swept across the country.

The very next year was the first of marches and protests that formed the Gay Pride parades of celebration and demanding equal rights. Who would have imagined that those early days were giving birth to a struggle that would take almost fifty years to be realized! LGBT rights are now a reality.

Reflecting back on my early years, I liked girls, but those relationships were few and far between. I attended Catholic schools for 12 years, and those influences framed my understanding of my sexuality. I eventually left the Catholic religious practice and I was "born-again" in a Baptist environment. It was too rigid, and I later found myself in a Quaker Fellowship. They were a peaceful, non-violent religious community, and I hoped to find myself a spiritual home.

Most of my life, I have been on a search for inner peace. It was from that spring-board that I pursued educational achievements to discover meaning and a way to help others. My degrees in psychology, while helpful, did not satisfy my nagging need of feeling complete.

The achievement of which I am most proud, was when my fiction works were submitted, and I received the Wallace Stegner Fellowship through Stanford University's creative writing program.

As to my first sexual experiences, those occurred in college. They were brief and affectionate, experiences over the next few years. There were no long term relationship involvements. I guess I expected them to be more satisfying than they turned out to be, and I was ultimately not happy with the experiences or with myself.

I had dated women off and on, and wanted to have children at some point. I was not sexually active with any of my female friends, and eventually gave up on the idea of a relationship that would produce children.

I moved to Oakland where I lived as a gay man until I was ordained in 1995

I have been celibate for 20 years since taking my vows. It is a daily challenge which is sometimes easier than others. My vows involve not only physical behavior but keeping my thoughts pure and focused.

As a monk I took vows of celibacy, and I believe I was always meant for living a private life.

I suspect in 20 years we will still look back with amazement at how our society views the gay community. In addition, I think religious communities are opening up to the common humanity gay people share.

I continue to work in areas of counseling and helping others to resolve their issues in their lives regarding sexuality, as well as spiritual direction. I am at peace on my path, and feel that I am where I should be."

CHAPTER 12

JUDY AND DARLETTA HORN
TWO SINNERS SERVING GOD
THIRTY-TWO YEARS LATER...

Darletta shares her story in her own words. "Not everyone knows they are gay from birth. For many, it is a journey that spans years, marriages, pain and regrets as they search for that happily ever after love connection. So it was with my story. I was born in 1943, just before the end of World War II.

As I entered my teenage years, I was trying to fill a void in my life, due to the early death of my father. In 1958, at age 15 I was pregnant and unmarried. My search for love led me to a lot of the wrong boys, and at age 18, I married and gave birth to my second son. Our marriage ended shortly thereafter. We were both too young to cope with marriage and two young children.

Within three months I was on the streets, homeless, with two young children to support and protect. A police officer directed me to the 'Sunshine Mission' in downtown Los Angeles. They helped me get back on my feet.

I got a job at Stan's Drive-In, where I met my second husband and also had my first lesbian relationship with a young woman who came into the Drive-In.

I had three more children, a boy, a girl, and another son whom I lost at 3 days old. My husband didn't work, so I was the one responsible for supporting the family. He wanted me to make more money and found an agent for me, and I began working as a topless dancer. I started stripping as a full time career, which gave him more money. It did little to support me and my children.

My husband was not only verbally but physically abusive. He used me as a punching bag on many occasions. As the physical abuse continued, I began to fear for my children's safety and made preparations to separate from him as soon as possible. I finally filed for my second divorce.

By the time I was 28 years old, I had been homeless, a stripper, abused, and was ready to find real love. I began to feel that I might actually be a lesbian, but had only acted on those feelings one time. While I was contemplating the lesbian option, I met Fred.

I entered into my third marriage with a good man who was willing to take on the responsibilities of four children and a growing family. I even told him that I thought I might be a lesbian. He assured me that he loved me and we would work it out. After six and a half years, although the marriage was a good one, I knew it was time to move on. I was now 35 years old.

At age 40, my life took a major turn. I met Judy Horn. Judy was the best dressed "man" in the gay scene, thirty-eight and single. She had no doubts that she was a lesbian and fully embraced the butch role. Judy believed she was born gay, and never questioned her role in life.

She told me that she had had her first lesbian experience when she was eighteen years old. She was with several women up until she was twenty-three. She was tending bar in a gay bar, and had tried being with a man; however, it didn't feel right to her. She knew her heart was attracted to women.

It was 1983 and Judy was 38 when we met, I was 40. She knew from the start that I was the one for her. She had a spiritual awakening and felt like God was leading us both into a life of ministry for Him.

Her journey from gay bars to ministry didn't really surprise her. She easily transitioned from the best dressed man in Long Beach to the best dressed preacher in the pulpit. When God called her to the ministry in 1992, we moved to Denver to start a church. Together we spent thirteen years in Denver at Christ Chapel of the Rockies.

We were two sinners serving God, and God became the focus of our lives as together, we learned to minister for Him.

About that time, there was a spiritual movement under way within the Christian gay churches. Rev. Thomas Hirsch felt that as more gay churches were emerging and being staffed by those who felt called to the ministry, but lacked formal training. He could help with the formation of Advance Christian Ministries. His vision was to travel around the country with a supportive network of teaching and fellowship.

This was a national meeting and teaching time for the ministers of smaller independent churches to come together for in depth prayer and fellowship. We joined with him, and soon we had begun to have credibility among pastors across the country. Each annual conference was well publicized, and all churches were invited to attend.

In October 1994, we were planning our meeting in New Caney, Texas at the Golden Cross Ranch with over 200 pastors from around the country.

What no one could have anticipated was a 100-year storm created by hurricane Rosa merging with a low level from the Gulf of Mexico. Texas was flooding, and all we could do was watch as the water levels began to flood the cabins of the conference grounds.

Judy and I had arrived early at the conference grounds, with about seventy-five other ministers. Suddenly, we were all in danger of being swept away by the currents. I worked side by side with Naomi Harvey and Tom Hirsch, directing everyone up to the cabins on higher ground. For over two days we prayed, and survived on what food we had rescued from the kitchen area. When the rains finally let up, our cabin was the only one not under water. We were rescued in small groups by two men in a small air boat, and all of us survived.

This was not true for many others during that flood. We are still grateful for God's protection. To this day, everyone who was there has a story to tell of the miracle that happened.

Symbolically, we have come through many floods since that time, and God has confirmed our calling into ministry time after time.

In 1993 our ministry had taken on another dimension when a woman came into our lives during an Advance Christian Ministry conference. She was proficient in American Sign Language, and was looking to train someone to carry on the ministry to sign for Jesus. I felt a stirring in my heart and began studies at the Center on Deafness in Denver, Colorado. I was determined to form an ASL group. This effort ended up as Praising Hands Ministry.

I also was determined to sign Christian Music and to teach others to do the same. Over the years I have ministered to the hearing impaired, as well as to the hearing congregations. At every church we were assigned, a choir was formed from those who wanted to worship God through Praising Hands.

In 1996 Judy and I prepared to attend the fall conference of the Alliance of Christian Churches. It would be held at the Patrick Henry Hotel in Williamsburg, Virginia. We were the first of the leadership to arrive, so they housed us in the Annex Building, next to the hotel. That building had only hotel rooms, but no other amenities.

We were getting settled in when Thomas Hirsch and two other friends came to our room. The other two visited only a few minutes, and then left as the plans for the conference needed to be finalized. When the others left us to do our planning, they failed to fully close the door. It wasn't more than 30 seconds before the door was flung open, and two men ran into our room. They were wearing camouflage jackets, and one was waving a gun. "Give us your money", they demanded.

I could smell alcohol on them, and saw that the one holding the gun was shaking. I remained calm and spoke in a soft voice. "Tom, take out your wallet. They want our money.

Tom complied, but only had one dollar in his wallet.

The man with the gun put it to Tom's temple, and then moved it down his neck. "More, more money!" He demanded "More money".

Judy turned to me and asked "Where is your purse?"

She said this knowing full well that all our cash was in her front jeans pocket. I only had makeup in my purse. I had just purchased new Estee' Lauder makeup, which we offered to the robbers. Thankfully, they didn't notice the diamond wedding ring and anniversary rings on my fingers.

They took my purse, jerked the phone cord from the wall, and said "Don't come out the door or we will shoot."

However, on the way out, they noticed Judy's briefcase which had several years of Alliance paperwork, along with our return plane tickets. They didn't notice Tom's briefcase which had several hundred dollars of conference money.

Tom waited a minute then started to open the door. I shouted, "No, don't do that. It's not safe." We started banging on the door with shoes and the telephone receiver. Finally, a security guard heard the noise and came to investigate.

The rest of the week was constantly interrupted as we looked at mug shots, to try to identify the robbers. We later learned that we were #3 out of 10 recent motel robberies. The men were picked up later that week, after they did in fact shoot someone, on robbery #10.

Judy's briefcase was later found by the railroad tracks behind the hotel. The paperwork and our plane tickets were still inside!

Eighteen years later, we are still amazed that God spared our lives and once again confirmed our call to the ministry.

In 2010 we moved back to Southern California where Judy served as the Assistant Pastor at Chapel of Peace with Pastor Linda McQuown. Advance Ministries took less and less prominence within the Christian Gay Community. As leaders changed, so did the face of smaller churches. The annual conferences still happened and those of us who had been called into ministry were acknowledged as ministers and set aside for the work of the ministry.

Many pastors came out of groups like the Metropolitan Community Church, or smaller start up congregations and often divisions of theology brought division of Biblical teaching. The national conference decided to disband, and the conferences on the west coast became ACTS West. The annual conference was shortened to weekends of worship and fellowship. Specific teaching instruction became the responsibility of the local pastors. More pastors from mainline churches, who had been kicked out, were finding support in the Christian gay fellowships. It appeared that God was doing a new thing, and bringing His word of love and reconciliation to the gay community. We were thrilled to be a part of this movement of God.

It was in June, 2010, Father's Day, when Judy and I were on the way to our church. She was scheduled to preach that morning. I was driving, while Judy was in the passenger seat finishing up her sermon notes.

We were transitioning on the 210 freeway and I put on my signal to merge to the "HOV" lane.

Suddenly a loud bang shattered our world as a black Hummer clipped our left tail light and sent us into an uncontrolled spin. Our vehicle slammed into the concrete median three times, bouncing like a ping pong ball. Our 2010 Honda Pilot flipped on its side and skidded about 200 feet. All 8 air bags deployed and sounded like rapid gunfire.

Neither of us could move with the seat belts and air bags holding us in place.

"Are you ok?" Judy asked.

My reply was soft, "I think so". We were both in shock.

Suddenly we were aware of voices outside the car. Judy counted fourteen people standing beside the car, counting in unison. "One - Two - Three" and suddenly our vehicle was up righted.

Later, one of the helpers who was a male nurse was asking Judy if she was all right.

"I think my arm is broken" She responded.

"Fold it against your chest until the paramedics get here," he instructed. It seemed like just a few minutes until they arrived and transported both of us to the hospital.

Judy had indeed broken her ulna and radius bones in her right arm. I was badly bruised, and one of my fingernails was actually ripped off. We were grateful for all those who stopped to help, and even more grateful that our injuries were not more severe or life threatening.

Snapshots of History Volume 2

Once again, I felt God has spared our lives that we might continue in service to Him.

I continue to build my signing choir called "Praising Hands", and it is reaching out to the hearing and hearing impaired alike. We are both active in the congregation at Glory Center in Bellflower, California, and together we are looking forward too many more years together. We were blessed to be legally married in California after over 30 years together.

Long term committed relationships are not unusual, and we are proud to share our story as one of the many couples who celebrate the fact that we are more in love than when we first got together.

The myth of transitory commitment is just that, a myth!"

CHAPTER 13

SUE BEAR LEBOW AND PATTY RHODES
32 WONDERFUL YEARS

S ue recalls, "Back in 1981 `don't ask don't tell' for the military wasn't a rule, but in the work place it was alive and well, even in a progressive state like California! Coming out happened behind closed doors, and women thinking they might be gay had no Google apps to clarify their feelings. Social groups like the Peninsula Women's Group in the San Francisco Bay Area were emerging as a place to meet other women. The group had weekly discussion meeting, weekend outings and dances.

On one of these trips to Mt. Whitney, four women in a three-person tent, Patty and I fell asleep holding hands, and the bombs exploding in our brains, turned out to be a helicopter landing at the summit of the mountain! That was the beginning of this unlikely Jewish girl and Catholic girl union. It would be 3 years before we rented the U-Haul trailer and moved in together.

Our history before that time was good preparation for a long term relationship. I grew up in a Reformed Jewish household with a dad who was devoted to his faith and a mother who didn't believe in anything, especially showing love and affection to me. My mother was repeating her own childhood, where she also was deprived of love. My mother didn't talk to me except when necessary, and she yelled about the 'idiot' who her sister should not emulate.

I was fearful of being killed during the night by my hateful mother. I lived through years of verbal and emotional abuse where my mother screamed at me, but never talked to me! We had several family members who suffered from mental illness, and my mom was always on the verge of crazy!

My grandmother was supportive of me; however, it didn't fill the void in my heart, or the longing for love. Somehow, it must have been my fault. *Was I that unlovable?* That question haunted me for years.

The families of my friends seemed to make room for me, and show me love, but it wasn't the same. I went years without talking to my mother. My communication with my father was always at his place of work never in the home setting.

I enjoyed school because it took me away from my mother's verbal attacks. Each summer, from the age of 5 I was sent away to camp for 8 weeks. I remember my summers in Maine as fun times when I was accepted and always had a few special friends.

One summer, due to my family moving, I was sent to a different camp where I didn't know anyone. I was bullied the entire summer. At one point, I was stripped of my clothing and thrown out on the deck. It reinforced my low self-esteem and devastated me further because somehow I felt I somehow deserved it. I did return to my beloved camp the following summer and continued going there until I was 20 years old, and the camp went bankrupt. The house rule was that I was not allowed to be home during the summer months. One summer I went to Europe for eight weeks and the next year, I worked in a factory outside of London.

After high school, I went to college in upstate New York and moved on to do my graduate work in Boston.

Regardless of my achievements, I couldn't shake the negativity that my mother's words had implanted in my spirit. When I was twenty years old, I had an epiphany while visiting the Swiss Alps I was viewing the snowcapped peaks and was hit with an incredible revelation. *It's not my fault!* Literally, out of the blue I knew I was not to blame. I chose to go into counseling about that time, which also helped me resolve the issues with my mother.

In my mid-twenties when I learned that my mother almost died from complications of a medical procedure, I decided to write her a letter to let her know the impact she had had on my life. Not surprising, my mother was upset about the letter, tore it up, and did not respond. I, however was moving on with my life.

When my dad became terminally ill, I had to talk directly with my mother, something I had not done since I was 12 years old. When I finally came face to face with my mom, we managed to have a short, simple, and superficial conversation. I have always likened it to the Berlin wall coming down!

In graduate school, I met the perfect Jewish boy who was getting his degree in psychology. We married and moved to Indiana where he continued his education. He was very devoted and deeply in love with me. In 1977 we moved to San Francisco, California to take advantage of new job opportunities. I took a job as a vocational evaluator for the Easter Seal Society.

I had a great boss named Cheryl, who was the topic of much office gossip when she and her "room-mate" would ride into work together, and spent a lot of time together. Some of the other workers thought they were gay but had not confronted them personally.

I didn't want to just assume, so I went to her and asked if she was gay. That led to a two-hour conversation in Cheryl's office about what it meant to be gay and what it might feel like. I was captivated by the stories that still had to be kept private. As I listened to these stories, my whole life passed in front of me, and I immediately identified all those feelings I had felt in the past. I always knew I was different, but had assumed it was because my mother didn't love me. I now knew it was because I was gay. A lot of things began to make sense for the first time, and in my enthusiasm for the new revelations, I went running home and blurted out to my husband, "Guess what I learned about myself today?"

He, of course, was less than thrilled with the revelation that I thought I was a lesbian.

Cheryl was a wonderful teacher about all things gay. She and her partner would bring in books to read, music to listen to, and took me to gay bars. I had my first slow dance with Cheryl's partner, Lyn. I was on a thrilling discovery of this new gay adventure.

A few months later I told my husband, "I want a divorce."

My husband ran to the kitchen and grabbed a knife.

I ran into the bedroom, and jumped into bed pulling the covers up around my head. Everyone knows that's how you protect yourself from an attacker! *He's going to kill me.* My heart was racing.

My husband came into the bedroom and held the knife out to me. "Here, just stab me in the heart" It was typical Jewish drama.

Not what I expected.

He decided to go to Boston to see his mother; I made plans to move to San Mateo from San Francisco. I took our new car, and left him the two cats, which he was allergic to! Then, I called to let him know I was moving.

As I was settling in to my new place, I spent a lot of time talking with Cheryl, and experiencing my obligatory first lesbian relationship. When that ended after two years, I created a list of qualities I wanted in a partner. My self-image was improving with each passing day. It seemed I was living up to my Hebrew name: Shanah Fagel: meaning Beautiful Bird. That was better than the similar Jewish term, Fagelah, which means a gay man!

It was during this time that I started going to the Peninsula Women's group in San Carlos. I met many lesbians, including Patty. At one of the dances, I thought that Patty was coming on to me. It was both exciting and a bit scary at the same time. The way Patty remembers "the dance" was that I was dancing so close I was leaving bodily impressions against her shirt! Patty had recently ended a 9-year relationship, and she wasn't sure she was ready for something new, at this point in her life. We decided to take it slow.

On the Mt. Whitney excursion, I recall seeing Patty take a grapefruit and rip it open to eat it. That scene was so exciting that it stilled my heart. My only experience with grapefruit was with a serrated spoon and individual sections, one at a time. This woman brought a new excitement to my life; however, it was 3 years later, when they rented a U-Haul to merge households. A common lesbian joke is "What do you do on a second date?" The answer, "Rent a U-Haul" and move in. We lasted past the second date!

Patty's ex is still an integral part of our extended family and we have developed a wonderful relationship.

Patty was a Southern California girl, having grown up in San Bernardino and attended an all-Girl Catholic high school. She had feelings of attraction for years toward other girls for years but never acted on them. After she graduated, she went to Santa Barbara Junior College and then transferred to San Francisco State, to prepare for a teaching career. She stopped going to church once she was out of her parents' home, and never felt the need to come out to her parents once she had girlfriends.

I have retained my culturally appropriate Jewish girl persona which is paired well with Patty's Catholic upbringing. If this union was made in heaven you would be hard pressed to know if it was a Catholic or Jewish heaven! I still proclaim with great enthusiasm, "It's been thirty-two wonderful years."

"Five years in, Patty was diagnosed with Breast Cancer. I remember thinking that if I lost her to cancer, I had the best five years of my life." Patty has now been twenty-seven years' cancer free!

Sue shared how she came out to her father in 1981. She recalls that his response was: "I guess that's what happens when you move to San Francisco." His second response was, "Do you hate me?" assuming that all lesbians hate men.

In the 4 years following the death of my father, I called my mother once a week to see how she was doing. The conversations were short, but the fact that they even existed was totally amazing. I related to her as I would any older woman, with kindness, but not as a mother. I once considered but quickly dismissed the thought of asking her mother why she treated me so badly all those years. Then, I decided I already knew the answer and it really didn't matter after all. My mother couldn't help it. She was a victim of her own upbringing.

Sue reminds herself often that: "I really like the person I am now." She paused thoughtfully, "What I didn't have in my own family, I have found with a wonderful family of friends and we have a good support system with like-minded women."

Patty and I have learned that it is important to communicate and acknowledge our differences. We are compatible, and when conflicts do come up, we deal with them. We have different abilities and celebrate them in one another. This truly has been thirty-three wonderful years and counting!

ONE OF THE LEAST
UNDERSTOOD AND
MOST INVISIBLE SEXUAL
ORIENTATIONS IS "BISEXUAL."

CHAPTER 14

YVETTE CANTU SCHNIEDER
A "B" IN THE GENDER ALPHABET

W hat first appeared to be another gay then ex-gay story of a woman finding and living her truth and speaking out against reparative therapy has turned into so much more. Like the peeling away the layers of an onion, a genuine and dynamic voice has emerged, turning the ex-gay message on its head.

Yvette was once a highly respected Christian voice against homosexuality. From her history as a policy analyst at the Family Research Council; as a director of women's ministry at Exodus International headquarters, working with Alan Chambers, and as a consultant for Concerned Women for America to working with various political groups supporting Prop.8 in California, Yvette became a highly sought after speaker as example of those who had overcome homosexuality through a strong faith in Jesus Christ.

In 1987 at the age of twenty-one, she had come out as a lesbian. Yvette and her girl friend were soon introduced to Glaad, and supported their work in southern California at the time. She "came out" to her mother and went through various experiences of disapproval, including one time being told to remove her commitment ring because her sister was bringing a boyfriend home from the East Coast.

"I refused" she stated. "She's living with him without a commitment, and I am proud of my commitment with my girlfriend."

When she "came out" as a Christian, she could no longer be open and proud about her sexuality, but quickly descended into shame as all the pastors she spoke with reinforced the idea that her sexuality was deviant and sinful. She believed their interpretation of certain Biblical passages because they were the "experts".

She worked in a college campus ministry, and began to "come out" about having been a lesbian. She was invited to tape a segment on a local Christian TV show with Joe Dallas, an outspoken ex-gay leader with Exodus International.

She was asked to speak at other events, and began to meet other prominent anti-gay figures. It wasn't long before she joined the full time staff at Family Research Council after Gary Bauer saw the short video she made proclaiming family values. They flew her to Washington DC for an interview and she started work a month later

This was prior to Tony Perkins taking over the reins from Gary who left in 1999 to run for the Republican nomination for President. Janet Parshall had a radio show and Yvette worked closely with her on several projects. She also worked with Bob Knight. He was a key contact in connecting Yvette with Concerned Women for America. Each of these contacts had a strong anti-gay agenda. Yvette was immediately on the front lines with them.

She was also a participant in briefings on Capitol Hill for several issues other than homosexuality.

Yvette became aware early on of the strong feelings that her colleagues had regarding gay marriage, LGBT equality, and the 'gay agenda'. Even in the anti-gay world there is conflict because of Christian beliefs that range from homosexual behavior being sinful to a deep repugnance of homosexual people. The attacks she heard from the pulpit regarding effeminate gay men in particular began to gnaw at her spirit. The preacher would talk about loving the sinner but hating the sin, and then follow it up with, "These aren't the type of people we want here anyway." The concept that a gay person could also be a Christian was not even entertained.

Yvette participated in several video presentations, which are still touted today as proof that homosexuals can change. She observes, "I don't think anyone was helped or encouraged to not be gay by our media presentations." The goal was to "sing to the choir" and draw attention to the small group of voices declaring they were no longer gay. She kind of felt it was her duty to champion Christian causes that supported family values, because each opportunity was offered as a way to help those who struggled with their sexual orientation. Yvette didn't feel exploited as she shared her story. At that time, she wanted to help people, believed it was a "chosen behavior" that could be changed.

The church teachings she had embraced were strict, and used manipulatively in order to persuade people to act and believe a certain way. But these people were "her family," and she didn't feel she could disappoint them or cut them out of her life.

In 1999 when she married Paul, her life took on a different dynamic. She had been a lesbian; now she wasn't. She was telling her story, and perhaps being married added a bit of authenticity to her story of a change of heart. In a way she was still "coming out" about something. Paul was her very best friend, and she was comfortable sharing the details of her life with him. The births of her 2 children added more credibility to her story of being truly 'ex-gay.'

She was seen as living proof that "change" really does work, and of course having a faith in Jesus Christ was a bonus. She is still sometimes quoted as a woman who 'overcame' homosexuality. Once a story is in print or on video, it can often go on forever. However, the truth is often more than one identifiable gender/sexual identification.

Yvette was increasingly uncomfortable with the events surrounding Prop. 8, and her involvement with the political campaigns against same sex marriage being tied to Scripture and church doctrines. It didn't compute with her own experience of family members who had long term homosexual relationships, or her ex- girlfriend who had been in a committed lesbian relationship for almost twenty years. They were normal people, living normal lives and being "family" in the purest sense of the word

She now believes her involvement with Proposition 8 rallies were dishonest. She had to repeat the same lines as everyone else and speak out on harm that she knew was not valid. "We all sounded like we were on the same page," however, Yvette knew the deception behind how the questions were formed, and the canned answers, all prepared in advance of each event. Her enthusiasm and support for pro-family work faded and she began to pull away. She could no longer say things she didn't believe in the core of her being.

Yvette made a lot of friends in the ex-gay movement and despite all the proclamations of change; she realized that she just did not see it happening. What did and does happen is when a person comes to terms with the fact that their inner life does not match confession of healing from homosexuality they've been making, there is deep guilt and a sense of failure and betrayal.

There is seldom support or acceptance of such people within the church, and so little within the gay community, either, so if they reenter the gay community, there is often ridicule and condemnation from both camps. There is a deep fear of exposure and failure. Many who have come out of the ex-gay movement are famous names, and their lives are anything but fantastic. They have to reestablish their faith, and many lose their families; and their church connections. They are in a new space as they discover that they truly are the men and women created by God, just as they are, and accepted for who they are. It is a journey. It is a whole new thing to go public once again, and everyone finds it difficult to navigate those waters.

In 2014, when Exodus closed its doors, Yvette knew another group would form because there are still many church people who believe in the possibility of change and believe it is their mission to proclaim it. But the truth is reparative therapy has left a trail of broken people in its wake. It doesn't work and the harm it does in those who have placed their faith in it is devastating. In early 2014, Yvette joined with nine former ex-gay leaders, in partnership with the National Center for Lesbian rights calling for a ban on gay conversion therapy.

In July 2104, Yvette Schneider was contacted by Glaad to "come-out" as it were, on a totally different level. Jeremy Hooper contacted her when he became aware of her newly published book**: Never Not Broken-** A Journey of Unbridled Transformation.

Once again she "came-out" in full support of gay rights and marriage equality on a national platform. She states that "she is sorry for the pain she caused so many by calling for a change of their sexuality as proof of their Christian faith." Yvette is committed to speaking out for the value of all people and full equal inclusion of everyone in our society. This is what she say now.

"Sexuality is fluid and although I am married to a man who is my best friend, many of my emotional connections are deep bonds with woman. I do not believe love is relegated to gender, and I feel everyone should be able to love and appreciate all people with respect and dignity. I am so over restricting sexuality to specific sexual activity. I am on a life journey of "coming out" as someone who loves without judgment or restriction."

Shouldn't that be the goal for us all?

INTER-SEX: INTRODUCTION AND GLOSSARY

A long with bisexuals, perhaps one of the least understood conditions on the LGBTQI alphabet is the "I" (Intersex) person. This is not the same as a Transsexual person who has the awareness that their gender identification is different than their physical body. They may or may not identify as gay or lesbian.

Gender is the combination of social, psychological, and emotional traits that classify a person as male or female or somewhere on the spectrum from male to female. Think for a moment of the variety of colors on the color wheel. Each color has many different shades that are distinct from one another, yet are part of one another. So it is with sexuality.

During the third month of a babies' development, external genitals form and are controlled by hormone production. It is estimated that one in every 1500-2000 births results in a child with ambiguous genitalia. These children are intersex.

One of the major problems is that Intersex conditions are wholly biological, and are different from gender (how a person identifies) and sexual orientation (who a person is attracted to).

In inter sexed inviduals, variation in the path of prenatal development of the reproductive system cause traits we don't usually expect in typical boys and girls.

There may be different patterns of the X and Y chromosomes (karyotype); gonads (the testes and ovaries), internal reproductive and urinary organs (uterus, fallopian tubes, bladder and urethra) or different looking genitalia. A child might be born appearing to be female on the outside, but having mostly male-typical anatomy on the inside. A child might also be born with genitals that are somewhere in between the usual male and female type of presentation.

In the past, doctors would perform "minor" surgery to correct the genital anomalies, often without even a discussion with the parents. If a child was born with two sets of genitals, and the penis was less than an inch long, they would remove it and "determine" the child was a girl.

Of course, this didn't address any internal presentations of male organs. Statistically, more girls were created through these surgeries, than boys. The parents were instructed to raise the child as a girl, which was all good and fine, until puberty! Such intersex persons may not be aware of their condition until they are adults. Some people live and die with intersex anatomy without anyone, including themselves, ever knowing of their condition.

Where the condition is more obvious, these individuals have too often been designated as mentally ill and emotionally unstable. They are often the victims of ridicule, bullying and physical abuse if their condition becomes known. The three stories that follow, Michel, Jo and Emily reveal the difficult journey and heartache of many intersexed persons. Much of this information is documented in

Kathy Baldock's book: <u>Walking the Bridgeless Canyon: Repairing the Breach between the Church and the LGBT Community, (c) 2014,</u> For an in-depth history of Intersex research and biology see Chapter 8 of her book which contains extensive information and research and mis-information that has been presented through the years. (It is available on Amazon.com or from Canyonwalker Connections.)

DEFINITIONS:

Androgen insensitivity syndrome (AIS) is when a person who is genetically male (who has one X and one Y chromosome) is resistant to male hormones (called androgens). As a result, the person has some or all of the physical traits of a woman, but the genetic makeup of a man.

Androgynous: A person who blends both male and female characteristics in their appearance.

Androgens may be called "male hormones," but don't let the name fool you. Both men's and women's bodies produce androgens, just in differing amounts. In fact, androgens have more than 200 actions in women.

The principal androgens are testosterone and **androstenedione.** They are, of course, present in much higher levels in men and play an important role in male traits and reproductive activity

DSD: the medical term for differences of sex development.

Gender dysphoria is a condition in which there is a conflict between a person's physical gender and the gender he or she identifies with. For example, a person who is physically a boy may actually feel and act like a girl. The person is very uncomfortable with the gender they were assigned at birth.

Gender dysphoria used to be known as gender identity disorder.

People with gender dysphoria may act as members of the opposite sex. Gender dysphoria is not the same as homosexuality.

Identity conflicts need to continue over time to be considered gender dysphoria. How that gender conflict occurs is different in each person. Some people privately identify more with the other gender.

People who are born with ***ambiguous genitalia***, which can raise questions about their gender, may develop gender dysphoria.

Genderqueer: A person who does not stay within the confines of masculine or feminine dress

Hypospadias is a condition in which the opening of the urethra is on the underside of the penis, instead of at the tip. When a boy is developing in utero, the penis begins to form in the sixth week of fetal life. Two folds of tissue join each other in the middle and a hollow tube is formed in the middle of the future penis. This tube is the urethra and its opening is called the penile meatus. As the skin folds develop to form the penis, any interruption in this process leads to the meatus being located in a location further from the end of the penis. The exact etiology for this premature cessation of urethral formation is poorly understood. In addition, the etiology of the often-associated abnormal downward curvature (chordee) is also poorly understood.

Intersex is a general term for biologically/physically not being strictly male or female.

Karyotyping is a test to examine chromosomes in a sample of cells, which can help identify genetic problems as the cause of a disorder or disease.

Mosaic chimera -Both terms refer to one organism with two or more distinct populations of cells

Ovotestis: a single reproductive organ that produces both sperm and ova, either at different times or concurrently

Pseudo-hermaphroditism- This is an outdated term for a condition in which a person has the primary sex organs of one sex, but develops the secondary characteristics of the opposite sex.

True Hermaphroditism. True hermaphroditism is a medical term for an intersex condition in which an individual is born with ovarian and testicular tissue

CHAPTER 15

MICHAEL: MY INTERSEX STORY

" I was born in the Canadian Province of Quebec in the 1970's. At birth, I was found to have hypospadia and undescended testes. It was decided that I must have some sort of medical condition affecting my genital development. Testing was immediately performed so I might be assigned a sex.

Karyotyping was performed and at the time showed 46XX, hence I was diagnosed with female pseudo-hermaphroditism and assigned female sex.

Physicians suggested having my genitals surgically altered so that they would more closely resemble female genitals.

My parents were told that I was essentially a "'different look-ing'" female and that I would never develop as a male. They were told that surgery to 'normalize' me would be the best option.

My father was full blood Navajo and never agreed to any surgical interventions. What he did instead was to raise me as what is known in the Navajo tradition as Nadleh. This is a child usually raised as the gender opposite to their apparent sex at birth. The Navajo tradition before the Christian influence actually had 4 genders. In some American Indian tribes, children were known as two spirited when their gender and biological manifestations were in conflict.

I 'knew' from a young age, that I was not like all the other girls. I am not sure when the first time was that I saw other little girls run around naked, but I recognized that I was different. It was very confusing to me and I learned early on that I could not ever be naked around anybody. I preferred not to be naked, and even with my immediate family I would take baths in my swim pants.

Without being told, my understanding of myself from early on was that, I very much identified with boys. I preferred "'boy toys'" and played with boys more than girls. I was a child of non-French speaking parents, which presented other issues with fitting in at school. I learned early on that I had to fight back just because I was different in the society where we lived. I usually just bullied the bullies and my friendships were few, none of them intimate.

When I was 8, I moved to Germany with my mother and my sister. My mother took me to a new set of physicians, who retested me. It was then that they found my genital appearance along with a few other oddities of my body as being inconsistent with my previous diagnosis. Those doctors determined that I actually had 46XY/XX mosaic chimerism. I was now diagnosed with "True Hermaphroditism".

This new diagnosis did not change my treatment or their recommendations to my mother in any way. It was as if they didn't even care that the child in front of them very much looked like a little boy. They didn't even bother to ask me how I felt about my body or which way I wanted to live my life. I was left with more confusion and unanswered questions.

I am not sure why it was the paradigm of John Money, (1920-2006) that it only mattered in which sex/gender a child was raised. Officially and on paper I was a girl, yet inside, that was not the case. My parents had just decided to go with what had seemed to be the best recommendation at the time. I do not know what formed their decision process; however, it wasn't working for me.

I was started on HRT (Hormone Replacement Therapy) at age 10. None of these interventions ever changed my self-perception as a male. In addition, I was now clearly attracted to girls, which presented another dilemma. I was probably around age 10 when I realized more conscientiously that I was 'attracted' to girls. The first time I remember 'falling in love' with a girl was when I was about 11 years old. Testosterone blockers were added around my 12th birthday in an attempt to correct my male inclinations.

When I was sixteen, I told my mother I was no longer taking HRT. I stopped taking the medications and let my body take over its natural order of things.

I soon developed typical signs of male puberty such as increasing body and facial hair along with a deeper voice. My peers had always seen me as a more masculine girl, and other than adolescent bullying, nobody really bothered me about my sexuality. I was an outsider all my life.

I soon realized that my desire to be involved with a girl would make it necessary for me to become somebody else. I embraced a male alter-ego and essentially I made up a story about myself and modified my first name to appear male.

I eventually wanted to find out if my hypospadia could be 'fixed'. I also wanted to know if the small vaginal opening which had no function in my mind, could be closed. It was very difficult for me to find a doctor who would understand my desire or even listen to my concerns.

I researched and found the top specialist on female to male surgery at the time in Germany. Because of his expertise in trans-sexual surgery, he was the perfect resource. He happened to practice in my hometown which was an added bonus. He examined me and he seemed to have no problem with performing the surgery. He also was the first person who was not concerned about my gender assignment.

At age 18 I had hypospadia surgery, but I still lived as a "female." It was later in my twenties that I officially "'transitioned'" and it was in the same manner any transgender would transition. But, it is important to understand that I am not a transgender person. It was very difficult to transition in Germany. I was in college by this time, studying to be a medical doctor. After I had completed medical school in Germany, I moved to California where transitioning was not as much an issue. One of the most significant issues is that I now present as male, but all of my degrees are from when I was female. Often it is assumed that I am transgendered.

I have ties to the Trans community, but I never felt I was a "'Trans'" man. I didn't quite fit in, again. A few years ago I finally connected to the Intersex community. I had no clue how many of us were out there. I am now advocating for intersex/DSD and I also am working on education for medical providers as well as the general population.

There is still a lot of mystery about intersex and differences of sexual development. I feel the more information that is available, the fewer stigmas there will be. Resources on sexuality continue to grow, and it is my desire that my life and personal experience will help not only the intersex community, but parents and medical personnel as they are confronted with this condition."

CHAPTER 16

JO

I 'm intersexed. There, I've come out and declared that, this is who I am.

I was born with ova-testis and a uterus. This is referred to as ovo-testis with disorders or differences of sexual development or OT/DSD. I also have testicular tissue, but it is not significant enough to produce testosterone. I was, however, incorrectly assigned male at birth. That has created numerous problems through the years. Personally, I have always identified as female.

I have always looked and sounded quite androgynous. I could assume the look of either gender. It was fairly typical for people to assume I was female. Sometimes they would ask what my gender was, and depending upon the circumstances, I would claim one or the other. There are actually over 30 differences of sexual development. DSD is the shortened method of identifying them.

I was born in a Navy hospital in Seattle, Washington, and raised in a Christian fundamentalist and strict military atmosphere. That, by itself is enough to cause conflict.

I lived with my biological mother and stepfather for the first 13 years of my life. My stepfather was in the Navy.

Since on paper I was a male, my feminine looks and nature seemed to irritate my stepfather. He frequently made it a point to physically abuse me into being more masculine. He was military, and he didn't want a sissy for a son. My siblings did not receive such treatment. My mother was oblivious to the constant bullying of my stepfather, and his physical abuse.

When I was about nine years-old, I began to seriously question my own sexuality. At school, students would assume me to be female. If anyone discovered that I was born a male, they would bully me.

I was abused at school and abused at home. I had no one to talk to regarding my confusion and no safe place to escape my torment. I struggled to maintain my grades, and they began to fail as I tried to deal with my sexuality conflicts. It was around the age of 11 that I began to go through female puberty.

I was absolutely confused and scared. I began to develop breasts. I was unsure of what to do, and had no one to talk to about my fears. I began to mutilate my chest, still never talking with anyone. I mutilated myself because I had thought that something was seriously wrong with me. One thing I knew for sure was that I absolutely couldn't let my parents know.

My parents also assumed that I had mental problems. So around this time they took me to the school counsellor, who suggested I might have a form of autism. It became clear to me that I couldn't talk to anyone at school either. This went on until I was 13. By that time, I was failing every class, and was being beaten every day at school. I was still physically abused at home, and deeply depressed. I often thought about suicide.

It was at this time that my biological father entered a court battle for custody of myself and my biological brother and sister. My grades were called into question, as was my "'health'". I had a small stature, and everyone attributed my being tiny to being unhealthy. I hadn't had any further testing around my DSD.

The lawyers interviewed my siblings, and when they learned that I was being physically abused at school and home, I was court-ordered to live with my father.

Nearly as soon as I moved in with my father I began having cramps. I complained about it to my father, but he yelled at me for it. He was also in the Navy at this time. "'Boys don't have cramps'" was his response. He was tough military all the way.

Although I was at a different school, and participated reluctantly in sports, I was physically and emotionally bullied by my peers as well at the teachers.

In more recent years as I have talked to my father, he said that he saw me as too weak for "'a boy of that age.'". He thought that all that I needed was a father figure who would help me to toughen up. It became his primary objective to "'help me become a man'." He forced me to get a hunting license, join wrestling, join football, and wear baggier clothes. Regardless of my very obvious physical issues, my father was in complete denial and still entirely focused on changing me to be a man.

They began teaching the endocrine system and female and male anatomy at school. I saw a lot of female attributes in myself, and also began to question why my gonads were different than what they were teaching. I was even more conflicted about my gender at this time.

My interests at the time were fashion, art, and nature. My dad did not like these interests, and when I would beg him to allow me to be more myself he would threaten to send me back to live with my mother and stepfather.

Once, I recall him taking me to McDonalds to have a talk. He told me that his entire extended family thought I was gay. Then, he said that he could not have his reputation tarnished for such a thing. He said that if I was gay, he would disown me and send me to a foster home.

We had been going to a church that fired my parents out of leadership positions because of me being too feminine for a "'boy' ". So, once again, my grades began to fail.

By the time I was 16, it had become completely apparent to me that I was physically different everyone else. I refused to take showers after gym or any of the other sports my father forced me to participate in. After gym, I'd often not even change out of my work out clothes. If no one was around, I'd change in a toilet stall. If other kids were still there and I was absolutely going to be late for class if I stayed any longer, I would just stay in my clothes.

I much preferred being bullied for wearing workout clothes to class, rather than to have them to see my chest and other issues that went along with female puberty. My hips were also widening.

It was also around this time that I had suspected I had one gonad that was, what I thought, missing. I tried telling my parents on numerous occasions. They ignored me, as they had all my life. I also had a lot of problems with massive migraines, physical exhaustion, and what I eventually found to be hot flashes. Now I know that was primarily because my estrogen levels weren't normal.

I assumed that clearly I wasn't meant to live. I began rebelling against everyone and everything. This was more than just teenage rebellion. I was being arrested on a regular basis for vandalism. I lived near a busy tourist facility and would often harass the visitors, but I never did anything violent. I also failed my 10th grade year.

Rather than listen to my concerns, my parents put me in a troubled student's class. When that didn't work, they gave me the option to go to a military academy or leave the house. I went to the military academy.

My tender chest problems seemed to calm down a bit at that time. But I was still feeling cramps on occasion. I was also a bit smarter at this time and knew for a fact that there was something out of the ordinary about my left gonad. I was taken to a military doctor, who stated that I had something interesting going on, but that it was no cause for concern. Later on, my stepmother took me to see someone who claimed that my cramps were caused by weak back muscles! I did make it through the school, though, although I was still conflicted about my gender.

Since then, it's been a cycle of moments when I would be seemingly doing alright then slip into deep depression. This continues to happen over and over again. I still have a lot of pressure from my family to be masculine and do what they think I should do to be who I need to be to satisfy them.

For me, my family's' acceptance of me has been a driving factor in everyday life. I eventually joined the Navy to gain their approval.

On multiple occasions, the Navy doctors had stated that my body was "'interesting'" but didn't feel it was any cause for alarm.

I just assumed it was normal and that migraines, hot flashes, and abdominal pain would always be an everyday thing.

In the barracks, I endured conversations like "'Wow Wilson, I wish I had your figure.'" or "'Wilson, you look more like a woman. Are you sure you're not?'" Several times I was told, "'You really should wear a bra.'" These were fairly typical comments about me.

We weren't allowed off base in uniform, so I had to change in the locker room. That was an absolutely dreadful daily experience! I hated that people stared at me and made comments. One guy even had the audacity to poke me and ask "'Why do you look so much like a woman?'"

But I dealt with the daily comments as best as I could. Inside I was dying. I began speaking to a therapist when I was about a year out from separating from the Navy. He claimed I had gender dysphoria. At least, I had a diagnosis, and could work towards getting a letter to receive hormone replacement therapy.

When I first spoke with my endocrinologist about HRT, he had said that he could tell straight away that physically something was off with me. It was another encouraging step toward fixing the lifelong problem.

I had blood drawn, and was sent in for a karyotype test. I told the doctor about my lower abdomen issues. At long last, someone was hearing me. I was sent to a specialist and had an ultrasound done. Four ultrasounds later, it was clear that I had ovarian tissue, failed testicular tissue, and an under developed uterus. The endocrinologist saw that I was not producing testosterone and I was given a low dose of estradiol to help relieve some of my hormonal problems. My current hormone levels are above average for most women my age. I was unaware of intersex definition at the time, but things started making more sense.

My family is still in denial about the things that happened with me when I was younger. It is like they are embarrassed that I am "'different'" and it's not just choices I am making. Despite all of this medical evidence, they state that they will only support me if I identify as male.

My sister has stopped talking to me entirely. She cannot comprehend how I can have this condition. The rest of my family refuses to support me because I "'socialize with homos and trannies.'" They say that those people will only 'suck you in and force you to join their clan.'" It hurts me that they will not become educated about the intersex condition.

At one point my stepmother had surprised me by saying that she feels sorry that I was born such a way, and thinks that I should do whatever is right. Shortly afterwards, she changed her mind and decided she couldn't embrace the fact that it was beyond my control.

Life has been very difficult for me. I'm honestly very surprised that I'm still alive. The intense conflict emotionally has caused many intersexed individuals to commit suicide. Many others have either been forced into surgery and hormone replacement therapy. Many just suffer mental anguish because their body is fighting itself. This is a hidden, often shameful, confusing condition and resources for understanding options are not always available.

Despite my body fighting itself, I've still managed to not have any very serious physical problems. I've been told that I can have surgery whenever I'm ready. I've managed to stay positive and focused through all of these years, and I don't fight depression as I did in the early years.

I'd say I'm extremely far behind in understanding my body and learning to deal with my condition. But being connected with the right people, other intersexed individuals like me, has without a doubt been the biggest help for me. There are support groups, web sites and physicians who are willing to work with me as I continue to understand my body. I don't blame anyone for being born with this condition. I don't understand why it happened to me, however, and I know I am not alone. One in every 1500 to 2000 births is an intersexed child.

I'm still not certain as to what my sexual orientation is, but I do currently have a very kind and loving boyfriend. I present as female, and I am comfortable with that gender identification. My boyfriend knows about my condition and continues to be supportive."

CHAPTER 17

EMILY- AGE 22 INTERSEXED

My name is Emily, I am 22 years old, and I have Partial Androgen Insensitivity Syndrome. Androgen insensitivity syndrome (AIS) is when a person who is genetically male (who has one X and one Y chromosome) is resistant to male hormones (called androgens). As a result, the person has some or all of the physical traits of a woman, but the genetic makeup of a man.

I was diagnosed at birth with "'Ambiguous Genitalia'". This term can be used to describe a number of Disorders of Sexual Development, or DSD. A blood test determined that I in fact had 46XY as my chromosomal DNA. My genitalia were neither fully developed male or female genitalia. My parents may have had to decide which gender I was going to be designated at the time I was born.

According to my medical records, which I read years later, I was phenotypical female with a male karyotype (46 XY). I still question to this day if my parents "'chose'" to make me female. According to what I was told, all the psychology and biology studies support that I would have felt like a female even if I had been raised as a male.

It was never explained to me what was happening, and I remember it being a painful process. My parents frequently took me to our doctor's appointments throughout my childhood. Vaginal dilation was performed on me from ages three to nine years of age. I never learned of my diagnoses and my intersex condition until the age of fourteen. It was an emotionally confusing time for me, and I didn't fully understand what it all meant.

I had always been told that I wasn't going to have a period like other girls, and I couldn't have a baby. That was all I really knew about my "'problem'" until I was 14 years old.

I didn't have problems making friends in my adolescent years. In middle and high school, I sometimes envied the other girls who were getting their periods. I was a happy normal girl most of my childhood. I played sports, had sleepovers, did all the normal for a girl my age. I didn't talk about my body being different, and was private when I had to change after sports activities.

It wasn't until 6th grade, when I was twelve, that things started to change for me. I began reading labels on food and tried harder in physical education class. My body seemed out of control.

Then in 7th grade about age 13, things went downhill fast. I developed an eating disorder, Anorexia Nervosa. It was an attempt to control the body I felt was out of my control. If I didn't eat, I figured I could just fade away.

I was admitted to an inpatient eating disorders program at a large university teaching hospital. The psychiatrist there in that program pulled me aside one day. His words were very technical and serious. "'Emily, you were born with XY chromosomes, girls have XX and *boys* have XY, you don't have a uterus, fallopian tubes, or ovaries'". My head was spinning with that information, trying to absorb his words.

I was already in a fragile state, and that information about did me in. I was devastated to learn how significantly different I was from every other female.

I had known my whole life that I was different. I just didn't know how different I was, until then. I was in shock and initially, I didn't handle this information very well.

I cried and felt horrible. I still do at times, especially when reading over my medical records. I would say that the blunt way the psychiatrist told me about my Androgen insensitivity syndrome, (AIS) only fueled my hatred toward my body even more. I felt betrayed by my own body at the core of my being.

Emotionally, I have experienced many problems in my life so far. I have been put on psychiatric medication in attempt to help me adjust. I suppose I was somewhat predisposed to have some emotional difficulties in my life. Learning how different I was from every other "normal female" just made things worse.

I am finally coming to peace with my condition. I have connected with other people who have similar stories, and it helps to know I am not alone. Sometimes though, I still feel so alone on this journey.

I think a key component for me will be finding a partner that loves me for me, despite my AIS. I am learning how to love myself and not hate my body.

That brings me to the question of sexuality. I identify as female and for the most part, I feel female. I look female on the outside, and I act like a female most of the time. I'm not sure where I really fit in my sexuality.

I was raised in a Christian home where boys liked girls, and girls like boys. It was understood that this was God's natural order of things. As a child I did not question this familial instinct. Then, around the age of 16 or 17 I began to find myself attracted to other females.

I didn't know why this was happening. I learned of the term "'lesbian'" and "'bisexual'" and I thought perhaps they really applied to me. If I didn't have all the right "girl" parts, how could I function as a female in life? Was it wrong for me to be attracted to girls? My inner conflicts around sexual orientation were in constant turmoil.

In my junior year at my private Christian high school, I went to a prom type event. I asked one of the sophomore guys to be my "'date.'" He reluctantly agreed, and we went to the prom event together. This was not your traditional prom. There was no dancing involved because that was seen as a sign of intimacy before marriage. Instead, we had a banquet, and watched a movie at a hotel. We then went to bed, there were no coed rooms. I actually felt happy during this time because a person I felt attracted to at the time was paying attention to me. That feeling was short lived, however.

The next day everyone went to an amusement park. Everyone was paired up just as they had been from the night before. My guy decided to ditch me and go off with his friends. I remember feeling rejected, angry, and sad. The old familiar thoughts consumed me. I'm not good enough for someone to care about, or love. I think I was angrier with my body for not being "'right'" than I was at him. A deep sadness emerged and covered my mind like a shroud. I am still on medication for depression, because I still struggle with mood swings and periods of deep sadness.

From that point on I started only imaging myself with women. I have had several relationships with girls in my life thus far. I still find myself attracted to women, although I am not ruling out the possibility of dating a man if the right one came across my path. When I am in a romantic relationship, I am very hesitant to tell the person about my AIS until I get to know them and trust them. So far, when I have told a person I was dating about my AIS, their response was very warm and understanding. I have found that most people are pretty accepting and trustworthy when it comes to information about this. I imagine only a small percentage of people are unaccepting of people with AIS or other intersex conditions.

When talking with medical doctors and other professional I have no difficulty at all talking about my Androgen insensitivity syndrome. I feel like the educator on this topic.

I have told maybe two or three "'friends'" about my Intersexed condition, but that was only after we became very close and I knew I could trust them. More often than not, I do find myself keeping it a secret. Since it is not obvious, there is no reason to "come out" with a declaration. Mostly, no one has betrayed my confidence.

My parents have been very loving about my condition since the day I was born. They don't know what to do at times or how to explain it, but they have always been there for me in terms of my AIS. To my knowledge, my parents do not think God made a mistake. I was born 3 months premature, so whether or not I was born on time or not I could still have AIS. I do not think God made a mistake.

I am angry at Him for making me like this sometimes, but I know He has a plan and one day this all will be put to good use. I have several role models in the AIS-Intersex community, and I aspire to one day be like them.

I know I can trust my parents as they have been supportive in the ways they know since the day I was born. When we lived overseas, they would fly me back to the states to see a specialist every so often. Although now I wonder if seeing all the medical professionals I did, did more bad than good. If I had not had all the surgeries as an infant, perhaps I could have chosen the type of surgery I want now, as a young adult.

There is a lot of discussion in medical circles about whether to "'correct'" the appearance of the genitals in situations like mine. There are over 31 intersex conditions and variations. This refers to the biology and /or appearance (phenotype) of an individual, where gender (how a person identifies) and sexual orientation, (who a person is attracted to) are all different things.

Intersex means a lot of different things for the individuals who are affected, from medical diagnosis, to sexual or gender identity, to a lifestyle. Gender as an identity is not linked to chromosomes, anatomy or hormone status as some would have us believe, it is an identity.

My identity is female, but an "intersex" female. I am still in the process of accepting my body for what it is.

EPILOGUE

I would be remiss to not share how the telling of these stories has impacted my understanding of gender and sexuality. Each unique voice has empowered me to be a more informed advocate in my tribe. My prayer is that we can see one another as human beings, without labels, and celebrate our connectedness.

There are many voices to be heard, all valid, and I am sorry I could not include them all.

I have grown in compassion, been saddened by the rejection, pain, and abuse many have experienced. I have rejoiced with those in long term committed relationships knowing the courage it takes to build a life with another person. I have a deep appreciation for what it means to be human.

Regardless of how we view ourselves and our sexuality, or lack of it, in the case of those who identify as Asexual, we are all loved by God, the Divine Spirit.

My journey continues to evolve as I live out my life as a senior Lesbian in a legal marriage. The laws of the land have changed, as have the attitudes in our society. We are not there yet, but I believe we are making inroads to understanding and acceptance.

Things I felt I understood as a teenager about sexuality, have changed dramatically. Love is not just between a man and a woman, it is between humans! What a concept.

We are all connected by Spirit, and we share this planet, with all our differences and similarities, gay, straight, bisexual, transgender, lesbian, intersex or asexual.

I believe as we learn to connect to one another, and share our stories, we become holy and more wholly and holy human!

I pray that your journey continues to be enriched by these voices. I know mine has.

Darlene Bogle
Turtlehrt@aol.com